THE BASSOON REED MANUAL
Lou Skinner's Theories and Techniques

On the cover: Lou Skinner in his home shop in Jonesport, Maine
Photograph by Ken Wagner

THE BASSOON REED MANUAL

Lou Skinner's Theories and Techniques

by JAMES R. McKAY
Contributing Authors RUSSELL HINKLE
and WILLIAM WOODWARD

INDIANA UNIVERSITY PRESS
BLOOMINGTON AND INDIANAPOLIS

PUBLISHED IN COOPERATION WITH

THE INTERNATIONAL
DOUBLE REED SOCIETY

This book is a publication of

Indiana University Press
601 North Morton Street
Bloomington, IN 47404-3797 USA

http://www.indiana.edu/~iupress

Telephone orders 800-842-6796
Fax orders 812-855-7931
E-mail orders iuporder

© 2000 by James R. McKay

All rights reserved

No part of this book may be reproduced or utilized in any form or by any means, electronic or mechanical, including photocopying and recording, or by any information storage and retrieval system, without permission in writing from the publisher. The Association of American University Presses' Resolution on Permissions constitutes the only exception to this prohibition.

The paper used in this publication meets the minimum requirements of American National Standard for Information Sciences—Permanence of Paper for Printed Library Materials, ANSI Z39.48-1984.

Manufactured in the United States of America

Library of Congress Cataloging-in-Publication Data

McKay, James, date
   The bassoon reed manual : Lou Skinner's theories and
     techniques / by James R. McKay ;   contributing authors,
     Russell Hinkle and William Woodward.
        p.   cm.
"Published in cooperation with the International Double Reed Society."
Includes bibliographical references.
ISBN 0-253-21312-6 (pa : alk. paper)
1. Bassoon—Reeds.   I. Skinner, Louis, d. 1993.
II. Hinkle, Russell, date   III. Woodward, William.
IV. International Double Reed Society.   V. Title.

ML951 .M35   2000
788.5'8192—dc21   00-040960

1 2 3 4 5   05 04 03 02 01 00

CONTENTS

PREFACE BY JAMES R. MCKAY		xvii
THE LIFE AND TIMES OF LOU SKINNER		xxi

CHAPTER 1 THEORETICAL PRINCIPLES AND CONCEPTS — 3

1.1	Apertures of Reeds	7
1.2	Reed Pitch	7
1.3	Resiliency of Cane and Fibers	8
1.4	Gouges	9
1.5	Aperture, Trim, and Voicing	10

CHAPTER 2 ESSENTIAL TOOLS FOR REED MAKING — 12

2.1	Scraping Wheels	12
2.2	Mandrels	12
2.3	Reamers	14
2.4	Shaper	14
2.5	Knives and Plaques	14
2.6	Files and Sandpaper	15
2.7	Pliers and End-Nipper	16
2.8	Rulers, Dividers, and Compasses	17
2.9	Wire, String, and Glue	19
2.10	Other Tools	19

CHAPTER 3 THE STRAIGHT TAPER REED: LOU SKINNER'S INTERPRETATION OF CARL MECHLER'S REED — 20

3.1	Preparation of Tubes, Gouging, and Profiling	20
	3.1.1 Split cane longitudinally into four parts	*20*
	3.1.2 Soak cane (the Sink Method)	*20*

	3.1.3	*Cut cane to length for gouging machine*	21
	3.1.4	*Cut off sharp edges (fillier)*	21
	3.1.5	*Gouge cane*	21
	3.1.6	*Profile cane (with profiling machine)*	21
	3.1.7	*Tie profiled cane to a piece of doweling*	22
3.2	Pre-Trim		23
	3.2.1	*Smooth and polish inside of gouge with 400 WD sandpaper; leave the dust, and polish with the smooth paper side of the sandpaper*	23
	3.2.2	*Shape cane*	23
	3.2.3	*Mark collar and wire positions*	25
3.3	Enhancement of the Inside of the Tube (Windsor Mill Process)	25
	3.3.1	*With pencil compass, mark the inside of gouge 32 mm from butt end*	26
	3.3.2	*Pilot cut*	26
	3.3.3	*Superimposed cut*	26
	3.3.4	*Sand entire inside butt with 200 DRY and 400 WD*	26
	3.3.5	*Define collar of reed*	26
3.4	Center-Panel Scoring	26
3.5	Parallel-Sides Pre-Trim	28
	3.5.1	*Mark blades and decrease thickness of profile*	28
	3.5.2	*Decrease thickness of blade sides by one-half to no thinner than 0.40 mm at edge*	28
	3.5.3	*Remove mid-range bump*	29
	3.5.4	*Pre-trim*	29
	3.5.5	*Sand entire surface lightly with 120 DRY*	29
	3.5.6	*Establish wings*	30
	3.5.7	*Eliminate pyramided fibers*	30
	3.5.8	*Sand pyramided fibers*	30
	3.5.9	*Re-establish fold line with knife-edge file*	30
	3.5.10	*Soak cane for 10 to 12 hours or until it sinks*	30
3.6	Forming and Drying	30
	3.6.1	*Fold and remove flare*	30
	3.6.2	*Side-slip top blade to left at butt by about 1 to 2 mm; pinch tip edge of reed*	31
	3.6.3	*Wrap reed starting at collar and proceeding to 2 mm from by butt end; finish with slipknot*	31
	3.6.4	*Place reed in hot water (90°C/194° F) for 20 minutes*	31
	3.6.5	*Insert the forming mandrel*	31
	3.6.6	*Partially unwrap string from butt end to just beyond wire III mark; put on wire III*	32

	3.6.7	Remove string and soak string in water	32
	3.6.8	With machine dividers, mark full fundamental length, the distance from wire II mark to tip edge, on the blade at 38 mm	33
	3.6.9	Put on wire II	33
	3.6.10	Butt molding	33
	3.6.11	Center-panel molding	33
	3.6.12	Retighten wires II and III and remove overlap on outside edge of cane between wire II and collar	33
	3.6.13	Narrow the tip edge to 15 mm if needed	33
	3.6.14	With knife-edge file, cut in adjustment notches (four or five) between wires II and III on center and sides of tube	33
	3.6.15	While reed and string are wet, put binding on reed	34
	3.6.16	File butt end of reed flat so reed can stand vertically	34
	3.6.17	Ream reed with drill and file reamers	34
	3.6.18	Straighten sides	35
	3.6.19	Cut reed	35
	3.6.20	Adjust side-slipping	35
	3.6.21	Clip corners of reed	35
	3.6.22	Smooth tip edge of reed if needed	35
	3.6.23	Put wire I on loosely between wire II and collar; slide it and secure 30 mm from the tip edge	36
	3.6.24	Tune the reed	36
	3.6.25	Apply two coats of glue	36
	3.6.26	Let reed dry	36
3.7	Final Stage		36
	3.7.1	Tighten wire II	36
	3.7.2	Tighten wire I	36
	3.7.3	Re-ream the tube	37
	3.7.4	Correct side-slipping	37
	3.7.5	Straighten sides, renew corners, and polish tip edge	37
3.8	Final Trim		37
	3.8.1	Tip undercut	37
	3.8.2	Blades	38
	3.8.3	Using fast-drying household cement or colored dope, paint binding of reed, ensuring that seal is re-established at wire II	39
	3.8.4	When glue is dry, soak reed for three to four minutes in water at room temperature	39

CHAPTER 4 THE TIP TAPER REED: LOU SKINNER'S INTERPRETATION OF KNOCHENHAUER'S REED — 40

- 4.1 Preparation of Tubes, Gouging, and Profiling — 40
  - 4.1.1 Split cane longitudinally into four parts — 40
  - 4.1.2 Soak cane for 12 hours at 20°C (68°F) or boil (for about one hour) until cane sinks — 40
  - 4.1.3 Cut cane to length for gouging machine — 40
  - 4.1.4 Cut off sharp edges (fillier) — 40
  - 4.1.5 Gouge cane — 41
  - 4.1.6 Profile cane by machine or by hand — 41
  - 4.1.7 Tie profiled cane to a piece of doweling — 43
- 4.2 Pre-Trim — 43
  - 4.2.1 Smooth and polish inside of gouge with 400 WD sandpaper; leave the dust, and polish with the smooth paper side of the sandpaper — 43
  - 4.2.2 Shape cane — 43
  - 4.2.3 Mark collar and wire positions — 43
- 4.3 Enhancement of the Inside of the Tube (Windsor Mill Process) — 44
  - 4.3.1 With pencil compass, mark the inside of gouge 32 mm from butt end — 44
  - 4.3.2 Pilot cut — 44
  - 4.3.3 Superimposed cut — 44
  - 4.3.4 Sand entire inside butt with 200 DRY and 400 WD — 44
  - 4.3.5 Define collar of reed — 45
- 4.4 Center-Panel Scoring — 45
- 4.5 Parallel-Sides Pre-Trim — 46
  - 4.5.1 Mark blades and decrease thickness of profile — 46
  - 4.5.2 Decrease thickness of sides of blade by one-half to no thinner than 0.04 mm at the edge — 46
  - 4.5.3 Remove mid-range bump — 47
  - 4.5.4 Pre-trim — 47
  - 4.5.5 Sand entire surface lightly with 120 DRY — 47
  - 4.5.6 Establish wings — 47
  - 4.5.7 Eliminate pyramided fibers — 48
  - 4.5.8 Sand pyramided fibers — 48
  - 4.5.9 Re-establish fold line with knife-edge file — 48
  - 4.5.10 Soak cane for 10 to 12 hours or until it sinks — 48
- 4.6 Forming and Drying — 48
  - 4.6.1 Fold and remove flare — 48
  - 4.6.2 Side-slip top blade to left at butt about 1 to 2 mm; pinch tip edge of reed — 49

	4.6.3	*Wrap reed, starting at collar and proceeding to 3 mm from butt end; finish with slipknot*	49
	4.6.4	*Place reed in hot water (90°C/194°F) for 20 minutes*	49
	4.6.5	*Insert the forming mandrel*	49
	4.6.6	*Partially unwrap string from butt end to just beyond wire III mark; put on wire III*	49
	4.6.7	*Remove string and soak string in water*	50
	4.6.8	*With machine dividers, mark full fundamental length, the distance from wire II mark to tip edge, on the blade at 38 mm*	50
	4.6.9	*Put on wire II*	50
	4.6.10	*Butt molding*	51
	4.6.11	*Center-panel molding*	51
	4.6.12	*Retighten wires II and III and remove overlap on outside edge of cane between wire II and collar*	51
	4.6.13	*Narrow tip edge to 15 mm if needed*	51
	4.6.14	*With knife-edge file, cut in adjustment notches (four or five) between wires III and II on center and sides of tube*	51
	4.6.15	*While reed and string are wet, put binding on reed*	51
	4.6.16	*File butt end of reed flat so reed can stand vertically*	52
	4.6.17	*Ream reed with drill and file reamers*	52
	4.6.18	*Straighten sides*	52
	4.6.19	*Cut reed*	53
	4.6.20	*Adjust side-slipping*	53
	4.6.21	*Clip corners of reed*	53
	4.6.22	*Smooth tip edge of reed if needed*	53
	4.6.23	*Put on wire I loosely between wire II and collar; slide it and secure 30 mm from tip edge*	53
	4.6.24	*Tune the reed*	54
	4.6.25	*Apply two coats of glue*	54
	4.6.26	*Let reed dry*	54
4.7	Final Stage		54
	4.7.1	*Tighten wire II*	54
	4.7.2	*Tighten wire I*	54
	4.7.3	*Re-ream the tube*	54
	4.7.4	*Correct side-slipping*	55
	4.7.5	*Straighten sides, renew corners, and polish tip edge*	55
4.8	Final Trim		55
	4.8.1	*OMIT tip undercut*	55
	4.8.2	*Blades*	55

| | 4.8.3 | *Using fast-drying household cement or colored dope, paint binding of reed, ensuring that seal is re-established at wire II* | 56 |
| | 4.8.4 | *When glue is dry, soak reed three to four minutes in water at room temperature* | 56 |

CHAPTER 5 VARIATIONS TO THE TUBE — 57

- 5.1 The Windsor Mill Process: Original Version — 57
- 5.2 Reverse Corona Variation — 58
- 5.3 Four Flats with Take-Out Variation — 59
- 5.4 Tube Taper — 60
- 5.5 Beveling Variation — 61

CHAPTER 6 VARIATIONS TO THE GOUGE AND THE INSIDE OF THE BLADES AND TUBES — 63

- 6.1 Linear Enhancements (LE) — 63
  - 6.1.1 *LE 22 reed* — 64
  - 6.1.2 *LE 43-50 (Charleston or Loonie) variation* — 66
  - 6.1.3 *LE 22-45 variation* — 67
- 6.2 The Dip Tip Variation — 68
- 6.3 Flute Gouge Variations — 69
  - 6.3.1 *Center Flute with eccentric gouge* — 69
  - 6.3.2 *Center Flute with inverted gouge* — 70
  - 6.3.3 *The Vivaldi reed (a variation of Center Flute)* — 71
  - 6.3.4 *Flat or elliptical Flute* — 72
- 6.4 The Sandboard Reed — 72
- 6.5 Even Down-About Shape (EDAS) — 73

CHAPTER 7 VARIATIONS TO THE OUTSIDE OF THE BLADES — 74

- 7.1 Aperture — 74
  - 7.1.1 *Aperture size* — 75
  - 7.1.2 *Tip-edge thickness* — 75
  - 7.1.3 *Aperture dampening* — 75
- 7.2 Voicing — 75
  - 7.2.1 *Tuning the reed* — 75
  - 7.2.2 *Adjusting the resonance of the reed: the rounded tube vs. the oval tube and the concept of presence in the sound* — 78
  - 7.2.3 *Presence and the differences between Mechler and Knochenhauer reeds* — 78
- 7.3 Troubleshooting: The Five Tests — 79
- 7.4 Additional Troubleshooting — 82
  - 7.4.1 *Popping the corners* — 82
  - 7.4.2 *Improving low D_1* — 82

CHAPTER 8	SPECIAL REEDS AND PROCESSES	83
8.1	The Del Negro Model	83
8.2	Offset Shape	84
8.3	The 1001 Sheherezade Reed	85
8.4	The 2001 Space Oddity Reed	87
8.5	Regular Oboe Trim	88
8.6	The Tabuteau Trim	88
8.7	Keeping the Flare on the Shape	89
8.8	Additional Sink Method	90
CHAPTER 9	A COMPARISON OF THE MECHLER AND KNOCHENHAUER REEDS	92
CHAPTER 10	THE CONTRABASSOON REED	97
10.1	Preparation of Tubes, Gouging, and Profiling	98
	10.1.1 Split the cane longitudinally into three parts	*98*
	10.1.2 Soak the cane (the Sink Method)	*98*
	10.1.3 Cut cane to 137 mm in length for gouging machine	*98*
	10.1.4 Cut off sharp edges (fillier)	*98*
	10.1.5 Gouge cane	*98*
	10.1.6 Profile cane (by profiling machine)	*99*
10.2	Shaping and Pre-Trim	99
	10.2.1 Making a masking-tape shaper template	*99*
	10.2.2 Shaping the cane	*100*
	10.2.3 Mark collar and wire positions	*100*
10.3	OMIT Windsor Mill Process	100
10.4	Center-Panel Scoring	100
	10.4.1 Define center panel and cut scores on tube ends	*100*
	10.4.2 Cut in collar	*102*
10.5	Pre-Trim	102
10.6	Forming and Drying	103
	10.6.1 Mark and score the center for folding	*103*
	10.6.2 Bevel cane	*103*
	10.6.3 Soak and fold cane	*103*
	10.6.4 Form tube	*104*
	10.6.5 Place wire III on tube	*104*
	10.6.6 Place wire II on tube	*105*
	10.6.7 Remove string and soak string in water	*105*
	10.6.8 File in adjustment notches	*105*
	10.6.9 Straighten the sides	*106*
	10.6.10 Wrap turk's head	*106*
	10.6.11 File butt end	*106*
	10.6.12 Ream the reed with the drill and file reamers	*106*

	10.6.13 Align sides	*106*
	10.6.14 Cut reed	*106*
	10.6.15 Adjust side-slipping	*106*
	10.6.16 Clip corners of reed and smooth tip edge	*106*
	10.6.17 Crow the reed	*107*
	10.6.18 Place wire I on the tube	*107*
	10.6.19 Glue tube	*107*
	10.6.20 Let reed dry	*107*
10.7	Final Stage	107
	10.7.1 Tighten wire II	*107*
	10.7.2 Tighten wire I	*107*
	10.7.3 Re-ream the tube	*108*
	10.7.4 Correct side-slipping	*108*
	10.7.5 Straighten sides	*108*
10.8	Final Trim	108
	10.8.1 Finish sanding the reed tip and blade surface	*108*
	10.8.2 Apply tip undercut (Darmstadt tip)	*108*
	10.8.3 Test the reed	*108*
	10.8.4 Adjust the reed	*108*
SOURCES		111
GLOSSARY		113

FIGURES

Figure 1.1	Reed nomenclature	4
Figure 1.2	Apertures of reeds	7
Figure 1.3	Cane fibers and vibration	8
Figure 1.4	Basic types of gouge	9
Figure 2.1	Scraping wheels	13
Figure 2.2	Mandrels	13
Figure 2.3	Fox #2 straight shaper and Exacto knife with #11 blade	15
Figure 2.4	Ruler, files, and drill reamer	16
Figure 2.5	How to fold sandpaper strips	16
Figure 2.6	Pliers and end-nipper	17
Figure 2.7	Dividers and compasses	17
Figure 2.8	Micrometer/dial indicator	18
Figure 2.9	Doweling dryers	18
Figure 2.10	Contrabassoon reed tools: brass template, #13 pin mandrel, 7/32-inch drill reamer, 5/16-inch file reamer, plaque	18
Figure 3.1	Side view of Straight and Tip Taper Profiles on dry cane	22
Figure 3.2	Cane being shaped	23
Figure 3.3	Feathered blades and butt end	24
Figure 3.4	Collar and wire marks	25
Figure 3.5	Cross-section of tube showing pilot and superimposed cuts	26
Figure 3.6	Sawtooth line on inside of tube	27
Figure 3.7	Center-panel scoring	27
Figure 3.8	Parallel sides and wings	28
Figure 3.9	Pre-trim beginning	29
Figure 3.10	Pre-trim wings	30
Figure 3.11	Partially unwrapping string and putting on wire III	32
Figure 3.12	Cross-section of tube at wire I, showing removal of overlap	33

Figure 3.13	Adjustment notches	34
Figure 3.14	Sapphire file on tip edge	35
Figure 3.15	Tip undercut	37
Figure 3.16	Final trim	38
Figure 4.1	Side-view of Straight and Tip Taper profiles	41
Figure 4.2	Collar and wire marks	43
Figure 4.3	Center-panel scoring	45
Figure 4.4	Parallel sides and wings	46
Figure 4.5	Pre-trim beginning	47
Figure 4.6	Pre-trim wings	48
Figure 4.7	Partially unwrapping string and putting on wire III	50
Figure 4.8	Cross-section of tube at wire I, showing removal of overlap	51
Figure 4.9	Adjustment notches	52
Figure 4.10	Sapphire file on tip edge	53
Figure 4.11	Final trim	55
Figure 5.1	Reverse Corona variation	59
Figure 5.2	Four Flats with Take-Out variation	60
Figure 5.3	Comparison of the Reverse Corona with Four Flats with Take-Out	60
Figure 5.4	Butt end of the reed with and without beveling	61
Figure 5.5	Beveling	61
Figure 6.1	LE 22 reed	64
Figure 6.2	LE 43-50 (Charleston or Loonie variation)	66
Figure 6.3	LE 22-45 variation	67
Figure 6.4	Flute gouges	69
Figure 6.5	Side view of Step 6.3.1, *Center Flute with eccentric gouge* (Steps 1 and 2)	70
Figure 6.6	Cross-section of cane in center for Vivaldi variation and top view of resonance-cut ridges	71
Figure 6.7	Flat flute (Section 6.3.4)	72
Figure 6.8	Top view of gouge for Sandboard reed	73
Figure 7.1	Diagram of reed to be used with the Five Tests	77
Figure 8.1	Offset shaping	85
Figure 8.2	Four Flats on the shape	85
Figure 8.3	Removing the shoulder	86
Figure 8.4	Regular oboe trim	88
Figure 8.5	Tabuteau trim	89
Figure 9.1	A Carl Mechler reed	color insert
Figure 9.2	A Wilhelm Knochenhauer reed	color insert
Figure 9.3	A Sherman Walt reed	color insert
Figure 9.4	A Ferdinand Del Negro reed	color insert
Figure 9.5	Lou Skinner's Straight Taper (Walt) model	color insert

Figure 9.6	Lou Skinner's Tip Taper (Del) model	color insert
Figure 10.1	Cutting off edges of cane	98
Figure 10.2	Profile for the contrabassoon reed	99
Figure 10.3	Contrabassoon reed shape	100
Figure 10.4	Double layer of masking tape folded over the brass template, with excess tape being cut away	100
Figure 10.5	Shaped masking tape placed on the profiled cane	101
Figure 10.6	Cutting in the collar	102
Figure 10.7	Undercutting the profile radius at the collar	102
Figure 10.8	Folding the cane with 1-mm side-slip	103
Figure 10.9	Placing wire III on the tube	105
Figure 10.10	One of Skinner's contrabassoon reeds, made in 1990	color insert
Figure 10.11	Detail of Figure 10.10: the same Skinner contrabassoon reed, enlarged	color insert

TABLES

Table 1.1	Effect of blade and bahn lengths on the "natural" pitches of the reed crow, assuming that the reed is 8.75 mm wide at the collar and 14.5 to 15.5 mm wide at the tip	5
Table 7.1	Natural pitches of reed crows, based on blade and bahn lengths	76
Table 7.2	Test 1, Tests for overall balance of cane in the blades	80
Table 7.3	Test 2, Tests for cane in the heart	80
Table 7.4	Test 3, Tests for cane in the mid-range section of the heart	81
Table 7.5	Tests 4 and 5, Test for thickness across the tip edge	81
Table 9.1	Comparison of Mechler and Knochenhauer reeds	93
Table 9.2	Comparison of Skinner's Straight Taper (Walt) model with his Tip Taper (Del Negro) model	95
Table 10.1	Effect of blade and bahn lengths on the natural pitches of the contrabassoon reed crow, assuming that the reed is 19 to 20 mm wide at the tip	97
Table 10.2	Measurements of one of Skinner's contrabassoon reeds made in 1990	109

PREFACE

There are two ways of teaching people how to make a bassoon reed. One way is to lay out a recipe to be followed step by step. The other way is to explain the principles of how a reed should function, giving the makers the information needed to create their own recipes. When we first went to Lou Skinner for lessons, most of us were taught different reed recipes based on his remarkable perception of what we needed to know at the moment. Gradually, as our lessons continued, we began to understand the theories that he had been telling us from the beginning, and began to apply them to the reeds that we were learning to make. For the book, however, Lou realized that the reader had to have the theoretical information, the recipes, and the applications all in one place at one time.

The chronology for the development of the book is as follows: from June 10 to 13, 1985, I invited Lou to give what would become the first York University Seminar in Toronto. He decided to present the Tip Taper reed. This was followed in 1986, from June 2 to 8, with the second seminar, on the Straight Taper reed. A few days before the second seminar, Lou asked me to write this book. During this seminar, and afterward, at Charleston Lake, Ontario, Lou and I started work. By December 1988, I had completed the first draft of Chapters 3 and 4 and had sent them to Lou for comment. During 1988 and 1989, I conducted "remote teaching," in which I tried various versions of Chapters 3 and 4 with my own students and then sent the results to Lou for comment. (The teaching was "remote" because, even though Lou could not be there, I made sure that his comments were communicated to the students and that he received their fees.) Until this time, we had toyed with the idea of presenting one basic reed recipe in the book. However, in 1989, Lou decided that we should be explicit about the two basic reeds, the Straight Taper and the Tip Taper, and that we should not try to make up a "generic" reed which could be transformed into either. He felt that this would better represent his interpretations of the Carl Mechler and the Wilhelm Knochenhauer reeds.

From August 9 to 19, 1990, Lou and I worked together on the book at Charleston

Lake. He kept emphasizing the "whys" and the "ifs," how the theory interfaced with practice, how the "variations" chapters should be presented, and what the overall shape of the book should be. I took countless pages of notes, made innumerable diagrams, and recorded over twenty hours of audio tape.

In 1984, Lou had typed up two documents: "Notes," six pages of theory, and "Excerpts from My Shop Notes," fourteen pages of diagrams. He had distributed these documents to his students from that point on, including students attending the York University seminars in 1985 and 1986. Chapter 1 is based to a large extent on those documents, and on his comments to me from 1986 to 1992, and especially from the summer of 1990. In 1992, Lou finally approved Chapters 3 and 4 and the outline of the remainder of the book—including the enunciation of the basic principles at the beginning of Chapter 1, the terminology in Figure 1.1, and a great number of other specifics.

In the summer of 1990, Lou decided that he wanted to include the Sink Method as an alternative to the Windsor Mill Process as part of Chapters 3 and 4. To give the reader a fuller picture of the flexibility in Lou's actual practice, I have inserted the full or double Sink Method into Chapter 3, and kept Chapter 4 the way Lou had approved it in 1988. In both Chapters 3 and 4, I have also included a modified Windsor Mill Process (which Lou approved) because of the freeing effect that this variation has on the vibrations of the blades. Section 5.1 now presents the *original* version of the Windsor Mill Process.

In August 1994, Bill Woodward, Gerry Corey, and I presented Chapters 3 and 4 at the International Double Reed Society (IDRS) conference, and in 1995 Bill Woodward received an IDRS grant to assist in completing the book. My deepest regret is that Lou passed away in 1993, before he could see the final product.

In a sense, this book is a summation of Lou's thoughts about bassoon reeds in the last decade of his life. It is not, and was never intended to be, a presentation of his fifty years of teaching. Those years will always remain gifts, given with care and love to all who had the privilege of studying with him.

There are many people whom I must thank for helping with the book. The first is "Snaggy," Lou's wife Betty Anne, who stood by him constantly until her untimely death in 1990.

Bill Woodward was Lou's last student and was determined to see the book finished. In a real sense, he is the "producer" of this project. Since his contact with me in 1994, he has been unswerving in his support and encouragement. He is the one responsible for obtaining the IDRS grant and for assembling Lou's biographical information presented in "The Life and Times of Lou Skinner." Bill also co-authored the chapter on contrabassoon reeds with Russ Hinkle.

Tom Elliot studied with Lou perhaps longer than any of the other students. I have often relied on his extensive memory and notes, especially for Chapters 6 and 8, to determine whether I had understood Lou correctly. Gerry Corey, Roland Small, Chris Weait, Ron Klimko, and Chip Kaufmann have also been generous in their help, as have

Sol Schoenbach, John Miller, Bradford Buckley, Don McGeen, and Greg Skinner, Lou's son. Per Hannevold kindly loaned me, for measurement, two Carl Mechler and three Wilhelm Knochenhauer reeds that Lou had given to him in 1993. I combined the measurements of these reeds with those of the two Mechler and two Knochenhauer reeds that I received from Lou to obtain the average blade dimensions in Table 9.1.

Research for this book has been supported by the Faculty of Music of the University of Western Ontario, by the International Double Reed Society, and by Minor Research Grants from the Faculty of Fine Arts of York University.

I would like to thank Georgia Law for manuscript editing and production, Bill Marks for digital photography, and Dan Homa for computer-based production of the diagrams.

Finally, my wife, Patricia, has been constantly supportive over the fourteen years it has taken me to write and publish this book. Lou and Snaggy loved her from the first time that we went to Jonesport, and she them. Patricia has continually reminded me of the deep love that Lou and Snaggy had for each other, and how their love enabled them to give so much so freely to so many.

James R. McKay
University of Western Ontario
London, Canada
2000

THE LIFE AND TIMES OF LOU SKINNER

"What makes a man devote his life to the study of reeds?"

Sol Schoenbach posed this question when reflecting on Lou Skinner's life. As the last edition of Lou's teaching notes boldly and proudly stated, he spent over fifty-four years making reeds. During that time he was greatly influenced by bassoonists he admired including Schoenbach and Ferdinand Del Negro of the Philadelphia Orchestra, and reed makers such as Carl Mechler[1] and Wilhelm Knochenhauer.[2] A partial answer to Sol Schoenbach's question lies in the fact that the secrets of reed making were not easily explained and not readily offered in Lou's formative days. Reed making was a mystery to be discovered the hard way by every student through personal trial and error. Lou's life's quest was to understand how the masters did it; as he came to unlock their secrets, he shared his knowledge with the hundreds of students who studied with him. In doing so, Lou Skinner became one of the greatest teachers of bassoon reed making in North America, and his influence has spread world wide.

Lou Skinner was born on August 28, 1918, in East Peoria, Illinois, to parents of English, Scottish, Irish, and Italian heritage. In this rural community, his start in music was typical of so many musicians, beginning with an opportunity in the public school system. Lou's first instrument was the clarinet, which he started to play at age seven. In 1929, his family (which included one sister) moved from East Peoria to nearby Pekin,

---

1. Carl Mechler was second bassoon in the Darmstadt Opera and manufactured excellent finished reeds. They were a straight taper style that Lou Skinner adopted as one of two basic styles on which he formed his theory and teaching (Chapter 3).

2. Wilhelm Knochenhauer was a bassoonist in the Dresden Symphony Orchestra and pursued the manufacture of tip taper style reeds, for which he became famous. Knochenhauer's reed style was the other basic style that Lou Skinner adopted for the basis of his theory and teaching (Chapter 4).

Illinois, where his father accepted a job as Deputy Sheriff. Lou continued to play clarinet in the Pekin Junior High School.

Lou's first encounter with the bassoon was at the age of fourteen, when he entered high school. Lou had asked to switch from clarinet to oboe. In one of those fateful events in life, the oboe was not available because the previous year's star oboe player had failed to graduate from high school and would be repeating the senior year. With the oboe taken, the band director suggested the bassoon. Upon reflection, Lou remembered the bassoon solo in a New York Philharmonic recording of Grieg's "The Hall of the Mountain King" and accepted the offer. The school's bassoon was an old 3000 or 4000 series Heckel with no whisper key. With some struggle Lou progressed to the point where, despite the Great Depression, the band director applied for and received funds to invest in a new Kohlert bassoon. Lou excelled with this new instrument, and when the Skinners moved back to Peoria in 1934, he continued to attend high school in Pekin.

At this time, Lou began playing in Peoria's amateur symphony orchestra. The Peoria Symphony played challenging repertoire including Scheherazade, Russlan and Ludmilla Overture, the Dvorak d minor symphony, and the Mendelssohn violin concerto. This connection with the symphony also gave Lou a chance to play in a wind quintet with the symphony's principal players.

While in high school, Lou planned to enter a local school music contest and searched for a good supply of reeds. He received some from Harold "Chappy" Cunnington, Principal Bassoonist with the St. Louis Symphony. Cunnington had studied reed making with Carl Mechler and made his own reeds, which were lighter than Mechler's. The reeds were well suited for Lou and enabled him to win both the school and state level contests. With these accomplishments, Lou took the opportunity to enter a national contest in Indianapolis that was judged by Vincent Pezzi. He received a "2" rating playing Weber's "Hungarian Rondo." Lou graduated from Pekin Community High School in 1936 as a National Honor Society student.

Lou Skinner's first professional opportunity came directly after high school, playing with Bohumir Kryl's forty-piece symphony orchestra. Kryl was a wealthy Bohemian trumpeter who organized his orchestra out of Chicago and drew top names from New York and Philadelphia. The orchestra barnstormed to points south and west including El Paso and Sante Fe. The musicians ate well and stayed in hotels, paying one dollar a night. The orchestra was made up of union members, but Kryl did not pay scale; this being the Depression, no one complained. Lou acknowledged that the main benefit to playing in Kryl's orchestra was the experience he accumulated. At the end of a tour with Kryl's orchestra in 1937, Lou ended up on the west coast. Staying with relatives, he played for seven months in the Bay Region Symphony, a WPA project orchestra.

It was here in San Francisco that Lou's reed-making career began, and it continued after he returned to Peoria the following year. He received a single reed lesson from Harold Cunnington, who did not even have a shaper. "Never mind," said Cunnington, "I'll do it with a ruler," showing an inventive spirit that characterized Lou's subsequent

1 Lou Skinner on tour with Bohumir Kryl's Symphony Orchestra

work. Cunnington's reed was linearly dampened—modeled after Carl Mechler's, but lighter. Through Cunnington, Lou was introduced to Carl Mechler's techniques for making both linearly dampened and laterally dampened reeds. Lou also took five or six bassoon lessons from Fred Innes (his first study with a bassoonist). Innes played on Knochenhauer reeds, and did not make his own. During this time, Lou worked at the Hiram Walker plant and played with the Peoria Municipal Band in the Majestic Theater.

In December 1942, Lou joined the Coast Guard and left Peoria the following March, bassoon in hand, for duty on the east coast. He attained a deep-sea rating for sonar and spent a year at sea chasing German submarines, a duty Lou regretted because of the human consequences of their success. In 1944, Lou got a call to join the Coast Guard Band in Curtis Bay, which provided him an opportunity to take on more pleasant duties. Lou had met his future wife, Betty Anne Hilton, in 1943, and during his years in the Coast Guard Band he played in a quintet with her brother Lewis, a clarinettist. Lou and Betty Anne were married on January 20, 1945.

Granted Wednesdays off from the Coast Guard for lessons, Lou met with Sol Schoenbach for the first time in Baltimore at the Lyric Theater, where Lou got his first lesson; subsequent lessons took place at Schoenbach's home in Philadelphia. Schoen-

2 *(above)* Lou Skinner and "Coasty" colleague Lew Kribel playing duets at Curtis Bay Barracks, 1944

3 *(right)* Lou Skinner played bassoon and contrabassoon in the Baltimore Symphony from 1946 until 1952

bach shared his Mechler and Knochenhauer reeds and the methods he had learned from studying with Carl Mechler. He also played a significant role in Lou's career by encouraging him to pursue reed making and research as a profession. When Sol Schoenbach was drafted into the Army, he advised Lou to study with his "great friend" Ferdinand Del Negro.

Lou first met Ferdinand Del Negro at the Philadelphia Opera, where Del Negro played in addition to his duties with the Philadelphia Orchestra. Bassoon lessons soon followed. Lou was particularly impressed with Del Negro's sound and staccato. While Del Negro did not teach reed making, he made them for his students to make sure they had good reeds on which to learn. Lou persisted in asking questions about reeds, and Del Negro would constantly drop hints, which Lou absorbed.

After the war ended and Lou was discharged from the Coast Guard, he remained in the Coast Guard Band until 1947, playing with Irv Goodman (Benny Goodman's brother), Tommy Dorsey, and Kai Winding. He also played recitals, the most notable being several with the cellist Felix Mendelssohn, grandson of the composer.

In the fall of 1946, the third bassoon and contrabassoon position opened up in the Baltimore Symphony. Lou aggressively sought the opportunity to audition. He first rented a contrabassoon from Bill Polisi in New York and then started lessons with Ferdinand Del Negro, who played contrabassoon for the Philadelphia Orchestra. Betty Anne went to the library and copied all of the contrabassoon solos from the works of Strauss, Brahms, and Dukas, and Lou played the audition for Reginald Stewart, using Del Negro's reeds. Having passed muster with Stewart on contrabassoon, Stewart then asked Lou to play bassoon. However, Lou had not brought his bassoon to the audition, which necessitated a hurried and anxious mile-and-a-half trip home and back (on foot) to retrieve it. Lou won the job and played in the Baltimore Symphony for seven seasons.

Lou left the Baltimore Symphony in 1952 because he wanted to make more money and to play with one of the larger orchestras. Illness kept him from auditioning for a position with the Boston Symphony Orchestra, so he turned to retail music sales to earn a living—first at Ted Martini's Music Shop in Baltimore and then at Beshore's Music in Belaire, Maryland. While working in sales, Lou was given time off for teaching, making reeds, playing with opera, ballet, and theater orchestras, and performing the full Gilbert and Sullivan cycle with Martin Green. During this period, Lou and Betty Anne lived in several houses, and Lou often named reed styles after the location where they were conceived. Thus the Windsor Mill method was devised during this period, when the Skinners lived on Windsor Mill Road.

In 1972, Lou and Betty Anne were traveling through Maine on vacation when they decided they wanted to live there. They looked for a house and found one they liked in Jonesport, a small lobster-fishing port near the Canadian border. In Jonesport, Lou pursued his reed making and teaching full-time.

Many students traveled to remote Jonesport to study with Lou. Students would either stay with Lou and Betty Anne or at "Tootsie's" bed and breakfast next door. Tootsie and Allan Beal (a retired lobster fisherman) provided excellent hospitality and were

4 Betty Anne did the gouging for the Skinner cane business

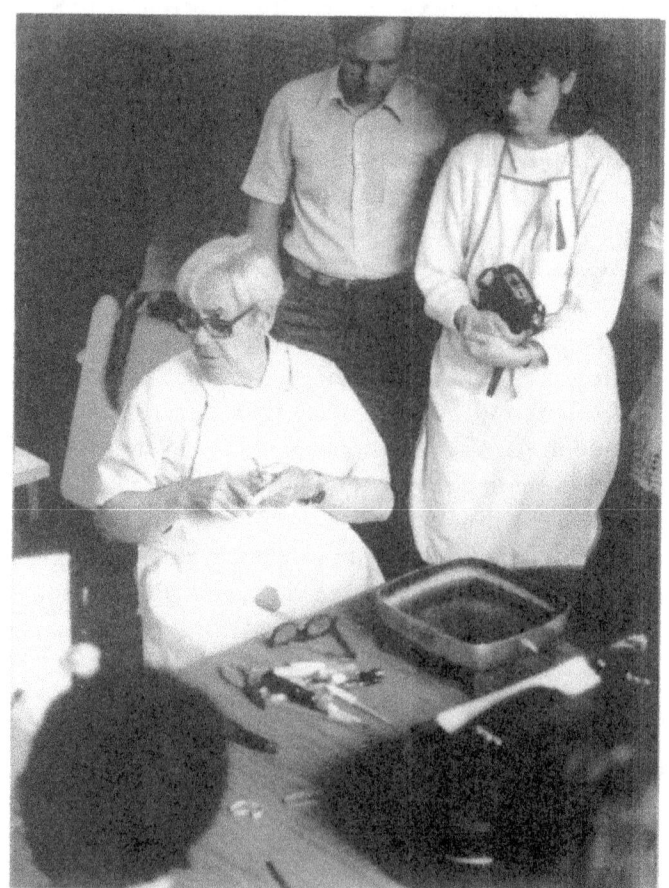

5 Lou Skinner teaching at the York University Seminar in June 1986.
Photo by Patricia McKay

6 *(above)* **Lou Skinner teaching his methods at the 1987 Miller/ Skinner Symposium in Towson, Maryland.** *Photo by Norma Hooks*

7 *(left)* **Lou Skinner having finished another great reed (May 1990)**

great neighbors to the Skinners. The standard lesson would run from three to five days. There would be three or four hours of work in the morning and another three or four hours in the afternoon; then it was time to enjoy the evening. All of Lou's students came to recognize Betty Anne as a fine cook and and first-rate hostess. After a good dinner, evening relaxation included walks to the harbor, drinks, conversation, and listening to music. In addition to teaching reed making and selling reeds, Lou and Betty Anne sold gouged bassoon cane. It was Betty Anne who did the gouging.

During the Jonesport period, Lou taught numerous reed seminars as well as training private students. He gave two reed-making seminars at York University, in 1985 and 1986 (*see* Preface). With his longtime associate John Miller, he taught in annual Miller/Skinner Symposiums at Towson, Maryland from 1984 through 1987.

Lou Skinner died on July 27, 1993. His lifetime achievements in reed making were formally recognized by the International Double Reed Society in 1994, when he was elected an honorary member with the citation, "Lou Skinner's exacting research into more efficient vibrational characteristics of bassoon reeds provided a clear rise in the standard of the reed-maker's art in America."[3] It is the purpose of this book to document a portion of Lou's experience and knowledge so that they will be available to those who did not have the privilege to work directly with him.

3. The Double Reed, Vol. 17, No. 3, Winter 1994 (Idaho Falls, Idaho: Falls Printing Company), p. 17.

THE BASSOON REED MANUAL
Lou Skinner's Theories and Techniques

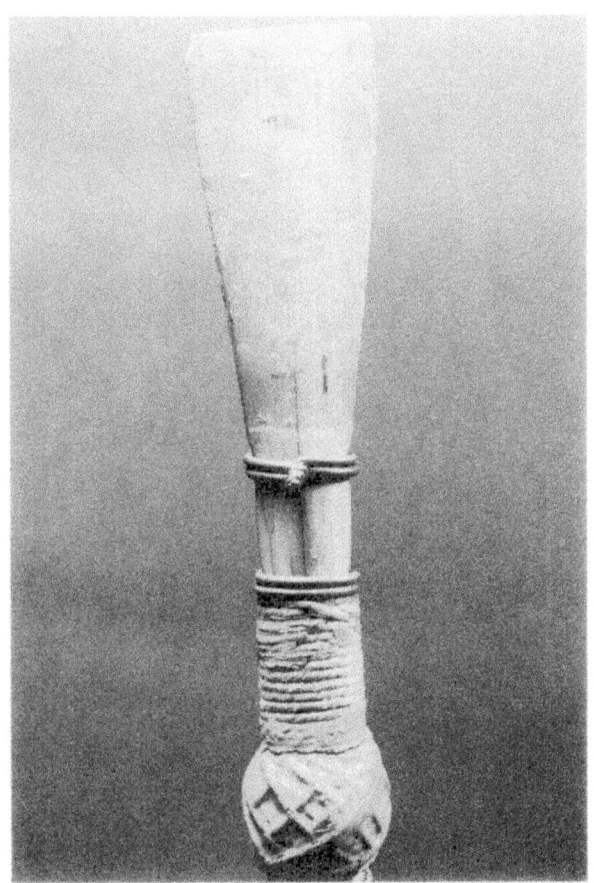

FIGURE 9.1
A Carl Mechler reed

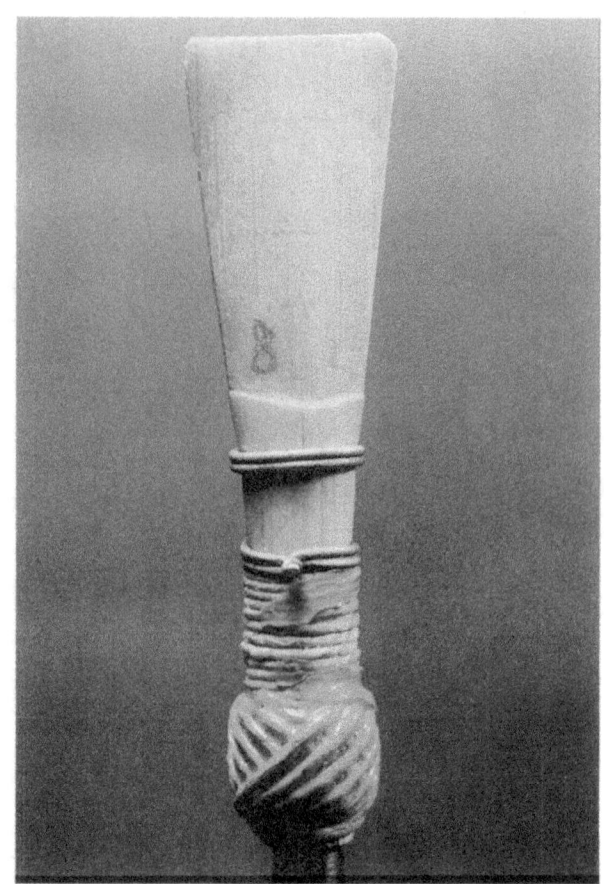
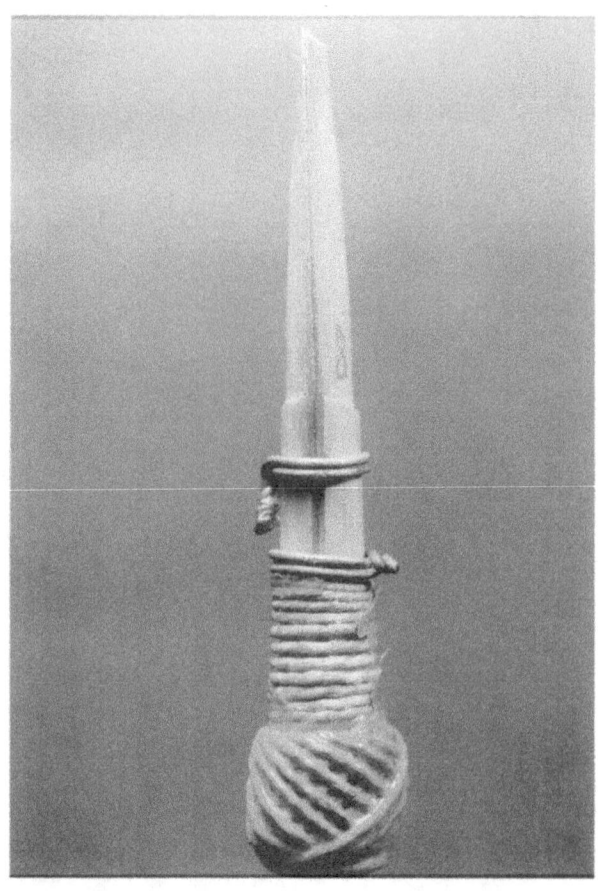

FIGURE 9.2
A Wilhelm Knochenhauer reed

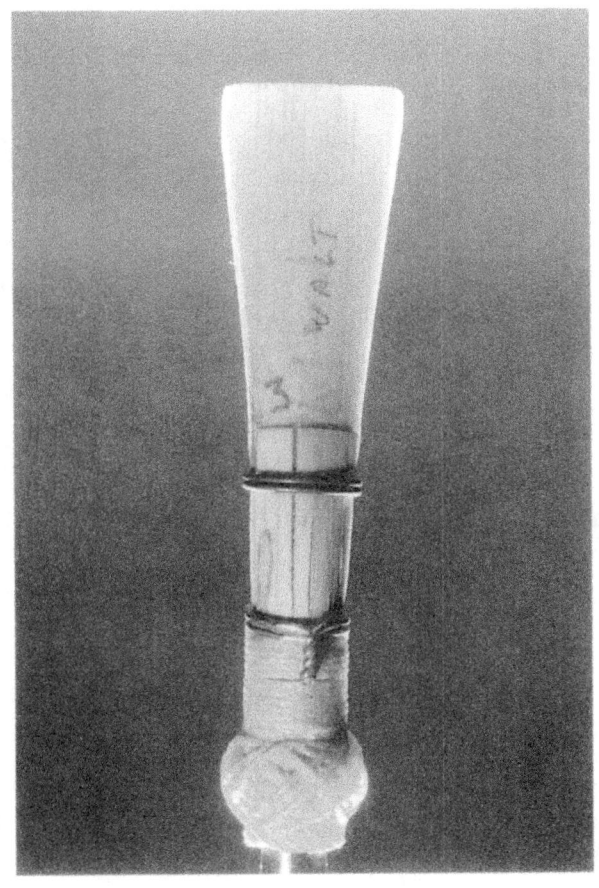
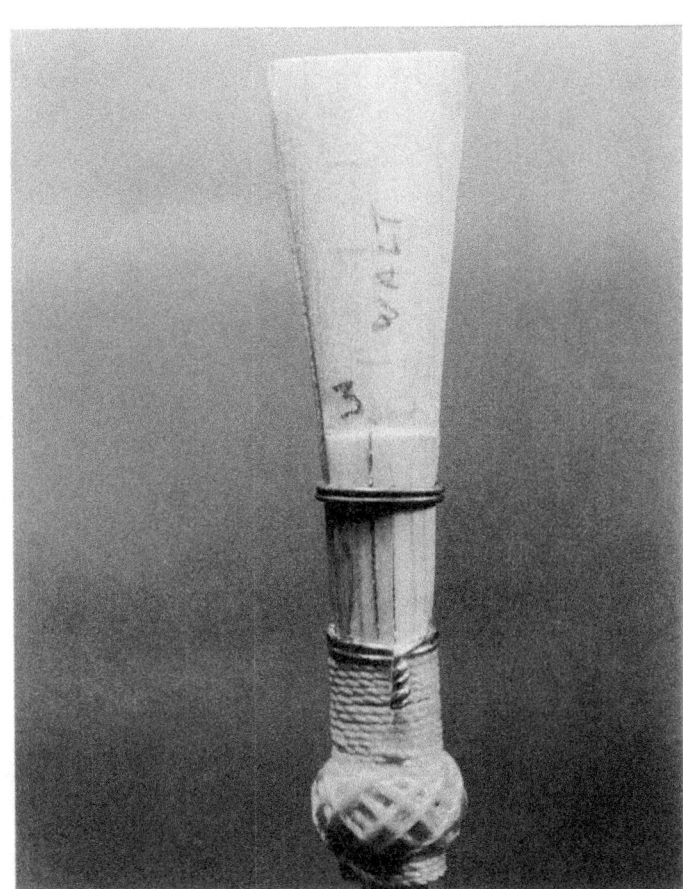

FIGURE 9.3
A Sherman Walt reed

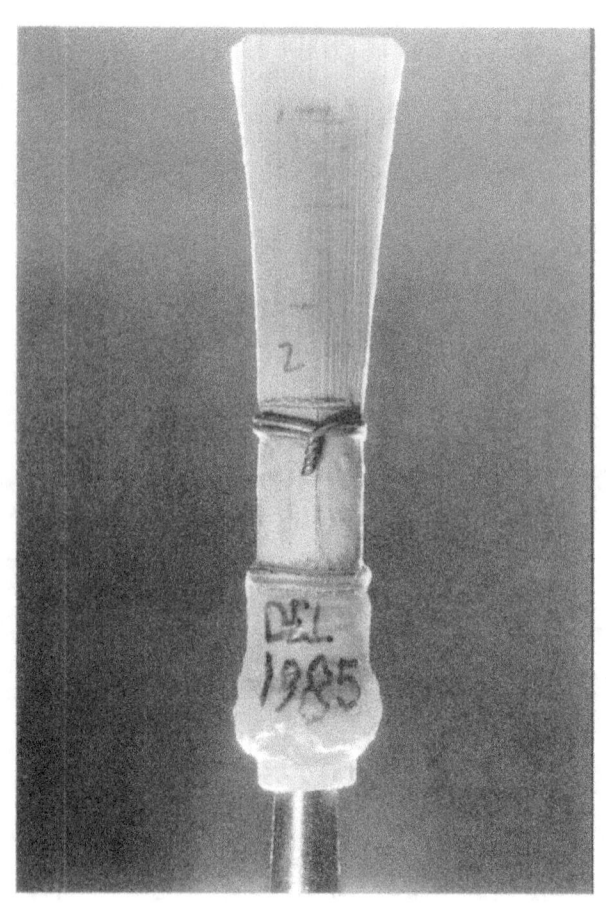

FIGURE 9.4
A Ferdinand Del Negro reed

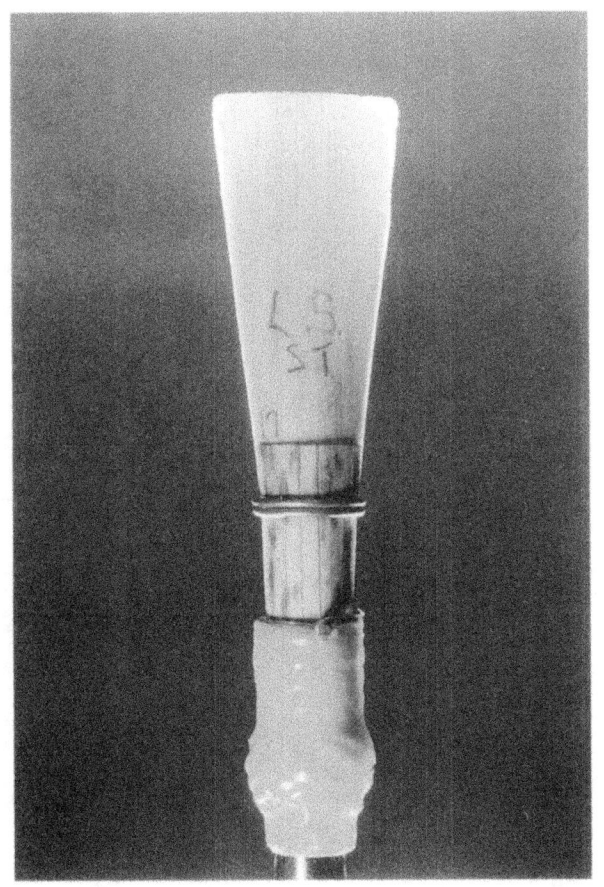
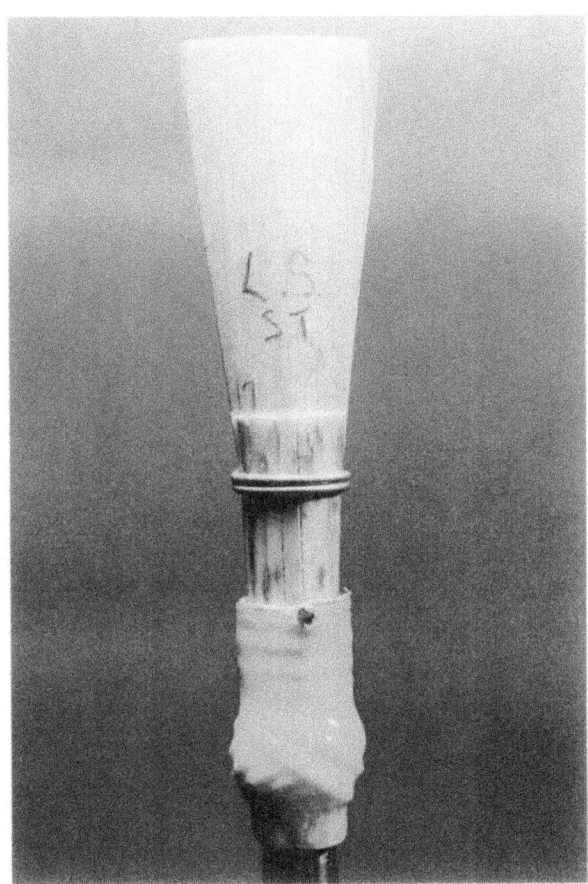
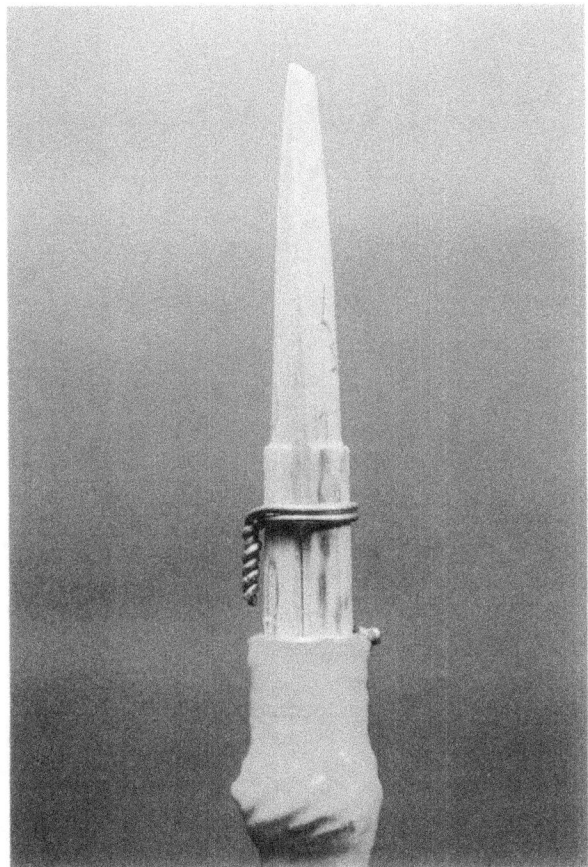

FIGURE 9.5
Lou Skinner's Straight Taper (Walt) model

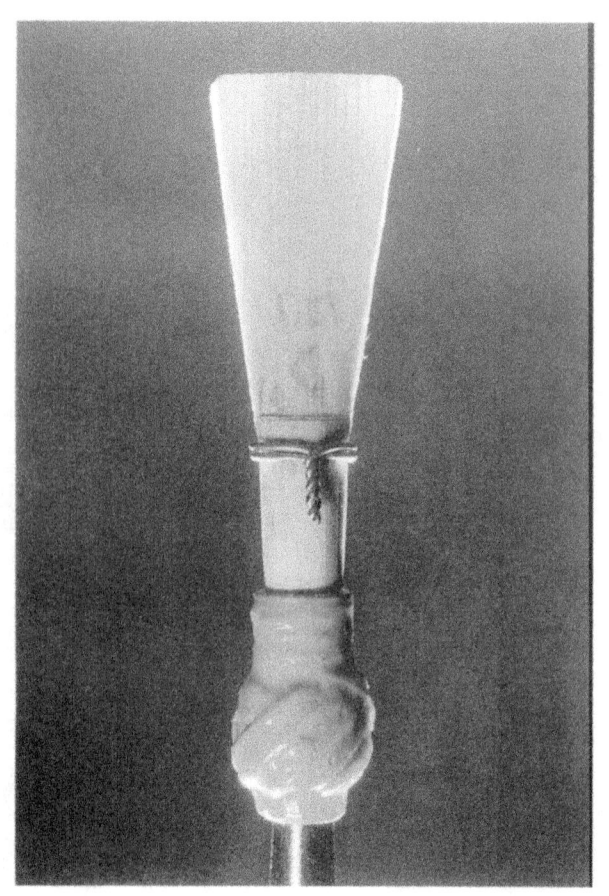
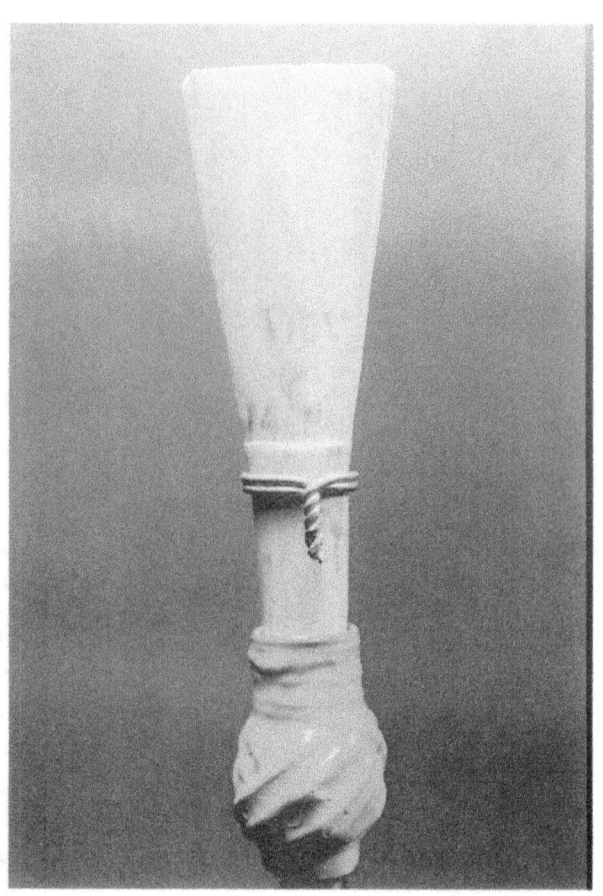

FIGURE 9.6
**Lou Skinner's Tip Taper
(Del) model**

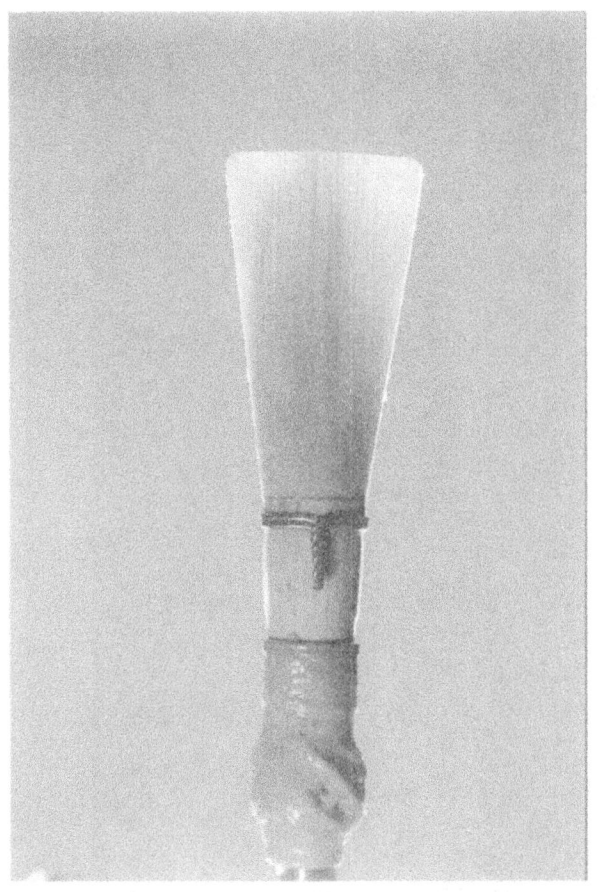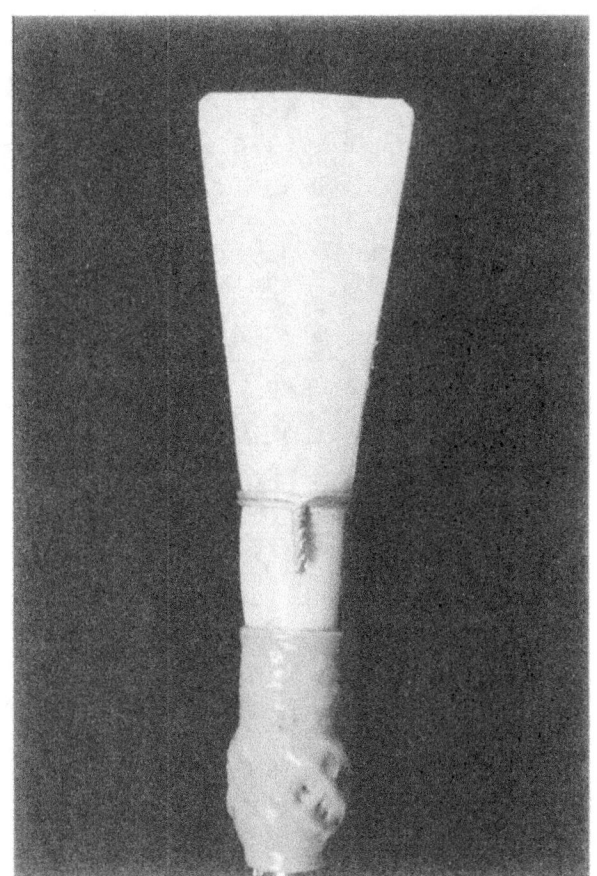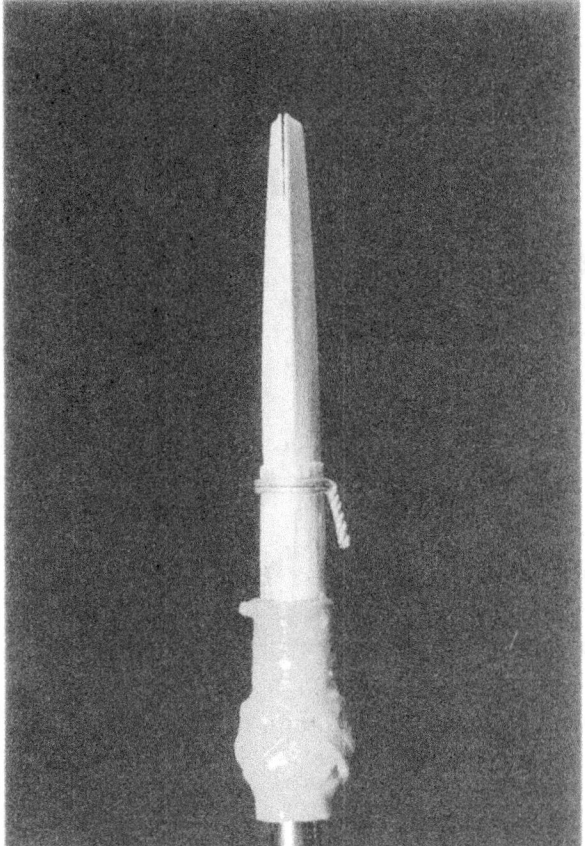

FIGURE 10.10
One of Skinner's contrabassoon reeds, made in 1990

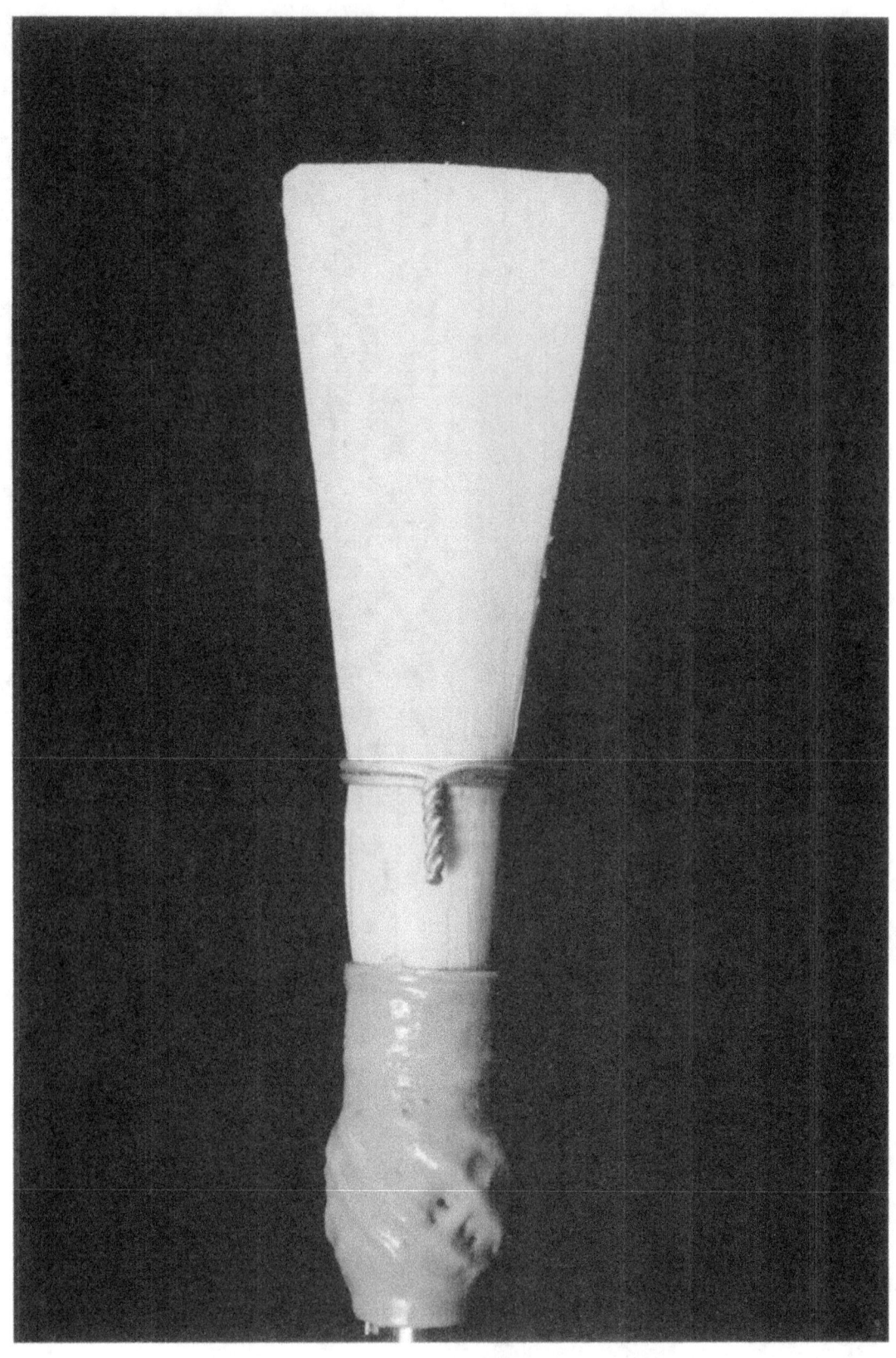

FIGURE 10.11 Detail of Figure 10.10: the same Skinner contrabassoon reed, enlarged

CHAPTER 1

THEORETICAL PRINCIPLES AND CONCEPTS

For over fifty years as a bassoon-reed maker, Lou Skinner never stopped studying reeds and thinking about them. He was the consummate researcher and became the consummate teacher because he always shared any discoveries with his students. Both his approach to reed making and his nomenclature evolved over his lifetime, so his more recent terminology may differ from what some of us remember from years ago. Figure 1.1 gives the nomenclature used in this book.

Skinner considered that there were two fundamental types of bassoon reeds, based on their physical structure and how this structure affected their dampening. The first type of reed, derived from Carl Mechler's reeds, has a *straight taper* profile and is primarily *linearly dampened*. Mechanically, "linear dampening" means that the greatest degree of dampening, or closing of the aperture by the embouchure, is achieved longitudinally—along the direction of the fibers, from the collar to the tip edge. This Straight Taper reed is presented in Chapter 3.

The second type of reed, derived from Wilhelm Knockenhauer's reeds, has a *tip taper* profile and is primarily laterally or *horizontally dampened*. Mechanically, "horizontal dampening" means that the greatest degree of dampening, or closing of the aperture by the embouchure, is achieved laterally—across the direction of the fibers, from side to side. This Tip Taper reed is presented in Chapter 4.

In a broader context, Skinner generally referred to changes made to the inside of the blades as linear dampening (**LD**) techniques (Chapter 6), and changes made to the outside of the blades as horizontal dampening (**HD**) techniques (Chapter 7). Therefore, both Straight and Tip Taper reeds have HD, but only Straight Taper reeds have LD.

Dampening can also be achieved by removing cane from the blades so that a slope is created through the layer of fibers. This sloping or *pyramiding* of the fibers, as will be explained in Section 1.3, can occur on the outside of the blades (Sections 3.5 and 4.5, and Step 7.4.2) or on the inside (Section 6.1). The simplest form of dampening by pyra-

4   Chapter 1

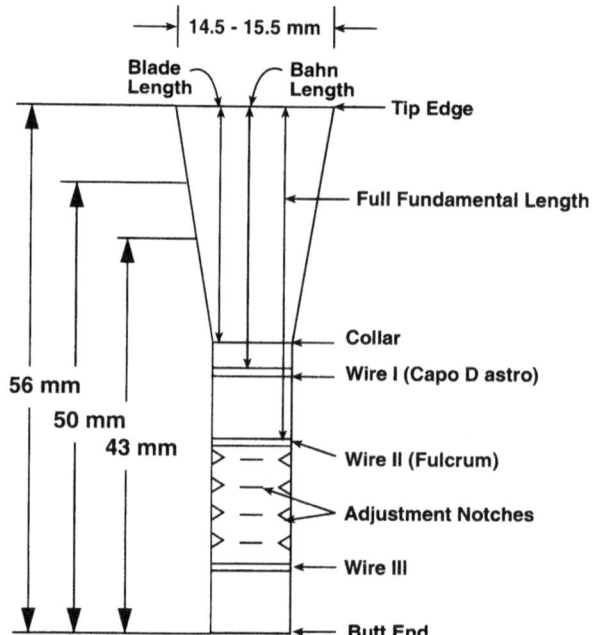

FIGURE 1.1
Reed nomenclature

miding fibers is the Tip Undercut (Step 3.8.1), where cane is removed from the inside of the tip edge on Straight Taper reeds.

Finally, dampening can be controlled by the wires and the shape of the tube. Tightening wire I will dampen the reed, as will making the tube rounder (Step 7.2.2, "Adjusting the resonance of the reed," and 7.2.3, "Presence and the differences between Mechler and Knockenhauer reeds").

The "natural" sound of the reed is determined by the *crow*, which is in three pitches, an upper pitch, and two lower pitches an octave apart. These natural pitches are determined by the blade and bahn lengths, as shown in Table 1.1. To drop the *upper* pitch of the crow on both Straight Taper and Tip Taper reeds, cane is taken out of the spine; to drop the *lower* pitch of the crow, cane is taken out of the sides, from in front of the collar to the middle of the blades. These points will be explained in detail later, but it will be helpful to bear them in mind as general principles.

The size of the reed (its overall dimensions) is governed by several factors:[4]

   a) The pitch at which the instrument was built
   b) The crook used
   c) The orchestral pitch to be attained

Some bassoons are built with a lower pitch than A-440, some are built on A-440, and some are built to a pitch higher than A-440.

---

4. Throughout the text, direct quotations from Lou Skinner are presented in bold type, without quotation marks. Emendations to his remarks are given in regular type.

According to the information Heckel furnishes about their crooks, the normal crook is the #1cc (or #1c). This crook will play at the pitch for which the instrument is built. Then there is a difference of 2.5 Hz lower or higher in sequence. For example, if the bassoon is built on A-440 and a #2 crook is used, the pitch of the instrument becomes A-437.5. This combination gives a darker quality to the sound, but it requires the player to raise the pitch to the orchestral pitch with embouchure or a sharper reed.

For this book, Skinner used 56 mm as the "standard length" of both the Straight Taper and Tip Taper reed, and he wanted both to have a bahn length of 30 mm, which will produce C as a "natural" pitch. He allows for a reed of 55 mm if the instrument/bocal plays flat. Nowhere in my experience does he discuss a 54- or a 57-mm reed, except for the Regular Oboe Trim Reed (Chapter 8.5). In the ensuing discussion, the reader must bear in mind that, although Skinner suggests different wire and collar placements, he always assumes a 56-mm reed.

In sharpening or raising the pitch of the reed, the FFL (full fundamental length) **of the reed, which is the length from the top of wire II to the tip edge of the reed, must be shortened. In shortening the FFL and using the same placement for wire I** (measured from the butt end), **the bahn length** (the distance from the top of wire I to the tip edge, as well as the blade length) **of the reed is shortened, thereby raising the pitch of the tuned fundamental.**

Skinner is implying here that the reed is cut shorter at the tip, thus shortening the blade and bahn lengths and raising the high and low "natural" pitches. The wire and collar measurements from the butt end have not changed.

A reed with a very short FFL (which produces a blade shorter than 25 mm and a *natural* higher partial above F) ***cannot*** **be tuned with wire I . . . the capo d'astro is not needed. Therefore wire I remains loose and must not be tightened.**

Skinner considered that in almost all cases, wire II served as a fulcrum, so that if you made the butt smaller by taking off the flare (Steps 3.6.1 and 4.6.1) or by applying a Tube Taper (Section 5.4), the aperture would be "popped" open. Conversely, if you made the tube larger by leaving the flare on, the fulcrum action of wire II would tend to close the aperture. Wire I therefore functions as a tuning device, or a *capo d'astro*. Its placement relative to the tip edge determines the blade and bahn lengths and, consequently, the "natural pitches" of the reed. Tightening wire I raises the pitch that the reed plays just after the tip has been clipped, and opening wire I with a #9 pin mandrel lowers the pitch (Steps 3.6.19 & 24 and 4.6.19 & 24).

The reed now has a basic fundamental pitch which must be made compatible with the fundamental pitch of the instrument; that is, whether the bassoon tends to play sharper or flatter. This can be done by adjustment of the embouchure and/or air pressure.

There are three basic pitches in the oscillation (crow) of the bassoon reed: the lows, mid-ranges, and highs (Table 1.1). The pitch of the highs can be varied by moving the point of embouchure. This allows the player a choice of the type of embouchure and placement of embouchure.

TABLE 1.1 **Effect of blade and bahn lengths on the "natural" pitches of the reed crow,[5] assuming that the reed is 8.75 mm wide at the collar and 14.5 to 15.5 mm wide at the tip**

REED CROWS HIGHS / LOWS	BLADE LENGTH	BAHN LENGTH
F / C	25 mm	30 mm
E / C	26 mm	30 mm
E flat / C	27 mm	30 mm
D / C	28 mm	30 mm
E / E flat	26 mm	27 mm
E / D	26 mm	28 mm
E / C sharp	26 mm	29 mm
E / C	26 mm	30 mm
E / B	26 mm	31 mm

The various pitches within the reed are governed by the
* Overall dimensions of the reed (Figure 1.1)
* Elevation of wires I and II, which determines the depth of the air chamber inside the reed
* Size of the trapezoidal vibrating surfaces (the blades)
* Placement of the wires with respect to the tip edge
* Capo d'astro effect of wire I
* Aperture of the reed in that the closer the tip edges are to each other, the faster and consequently higher the pitch of the oscillation

With reference to the last two points above, the pitch of the reed can be raised by closing the aperture with the embouchure, by changing the air pressure, and/or by flattening or tightening wire I.

There are three pitch adjustments necessary throughout the range of the instrument. I think most players will agree that we have to relax (and sometimes move) the point at which **the embouchure** touches the reed **to play the bass register in tune**, and a bit more embouchure pressure to play the extreme high register above high c^1.[6] There is, however, **no change** or little change, relatively speaking, in embouchure pressure to play from low F_1 natural to high c^1, therefore allowing **the pitch of the reed to remain con-**

---

5. In the document presented at the 1994 IDRS Conference, this table was incorrectly displayed. Table 1.1 gives the correct version.

6. Skinner assumes that the three registers of the bassoon are from B flat$_2$ to F_1, from F_1 to c^1, and from c^1 up.

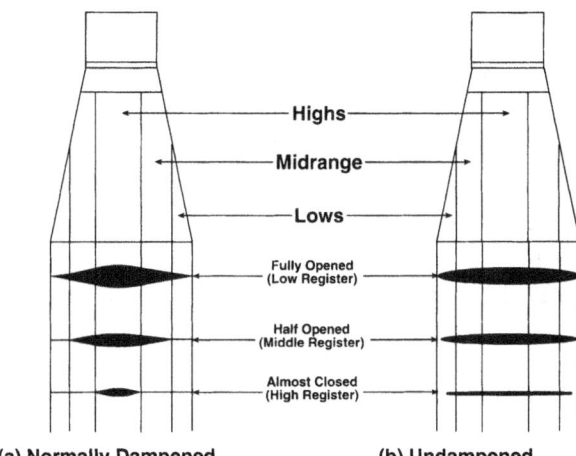

FIGURE 1.2
Apertures of reeds

stant over this range. The reed, when properly played, is somewhat lower in pitch for the bass register and somewhat higher in pitch for the extreme high register.

1.1 APERTURES OF REEDS

As seen in Figure 1.2, **there are two types of apertures: dampened and undampened.** The difference between a dampened aperture and an undampened aperture is that the sides of the tip edge (the edge of the reed in the mid-range and low areas) are farther apart in an undampened aperture than in a dampened aperture. The most open aperture is used when the player is playing low F_1 and below. A slight increase in embouchure pressure needed for the mid-range from low F_1 to high c^1 would produce a middle aperture, *half-opened*. This means that the player *dampens out* the low or wing areas of the reed at the aperture when playing in the middle register. Likewise, the most embouchure pressure is used for playing in the high register, when the performer *dampens out* the low- and mid-range areas of the reed and literally uses just the center of the reed at the aperture. Skinner's concept on how we dampen the reed as we play in the different registers is essential to the following section on the pitch areas of the reed blade and, indeed, for understanding internal variations to the blades discussed in Chapter 6.

1.2 REED PITCH

A reed produces its "natural" pitches when *crowed*, but you can change the pitches or tune the reed. Skinner's advice in this section will become critical later, since these reed pitches directly affect whether the bassoon plays sharp or flat (Section 7.2, *Voicing*).

The pitch of the highs is controlled by the length of the backbone (the length of the blade) and by the density of the cane in the backbone. This pitch is *the most stable*.

The pitch of the lows is controlled by the width, length, and density of the cane in the wings.

The pitch of the mid-range, which is an octave above the lows, is controlled by the width, length, and density of the cane in the mid-range portion of the blades, that portion located between the wings and the backbone on both sides of the blade. The mid-range can also cause the lows to vary in pitch ("*No Man's Land*").[7]

Highs, lows, and mid-range are all affected by the capo d'astro effect of wire I.

In addition, the Tip Taper reed described at Section 8.1 is Skinner's version of Del Negro's and Knochenhauer's reeds. The blade on Skinner's Del Negro (Tip Taper) model is 26 mm and the bahn 27 mm (Table 9.2). Therefore, the natural pitches according to Table 1.1 are E and E flat. Since the "crow" pitches that work best for most bassoons are E or F and B or C, the mid-range and lower pitches are far too high. Skinner (and Del Negro) therefore advised us to take cane out of "No Man's Land," the mid-range area, from 43 mm to the collar. In other words, by making the sides in front of the collar *razor thin* and extending the cane removal laterally into the blades, we took out enough cane from "No Man's Land" to drop the mid-range and low pitches of the reed to an acceptable C or B.

1.3 RESILIENCY OF CANE AND FIBERS

Each reed must be treated as a separate entity because each piece of cane is a separate entity. No two pieces are identical in size (curvature) and density, even if they are from the same tube. Two types of fibers must be considered: pyramided fibers (more resilient and more resistant to vibration) and parallel fibers (less resilient and less resistant to vibration).

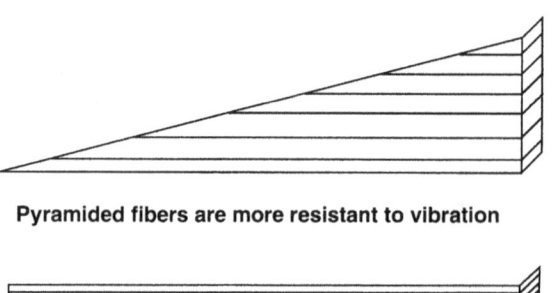

FIGURE 1.3 **Cane fibers and vibration**

Of course, Skinner is speaking here of the fibers of the blades after profiling. Comparing the Straight Taper reed and the Tip Taper reed, we find a difference in *resiliency*. In the Tip Taper reed, several layers of fiber are cut through at an angle, or *pyramided* (Figure 1.3). This pyramiding is found more in the front part of the reed, nearest the tip; the cuts in the back part of the reed, nearest the collar, tend to run parallel to the fibers. This means that the resistance to vibration in a Tip Taper reed will be greater in the pyramided area near the tip, and less in the parallel area nearer the collar. In the Straight Taper reed, the fibers are pyramided more or less evenly from the tip edge to the collar, and the resistance to vibration is more evenly distributed over the blades.

---

7. "No Man's Land" was Skinner's term for the back parts of the reed, from the collar to 43 mm on either side of the backbone.

The natural resiliency of the cane is an important consideration. The larger the original tube of cane is in diameter, the weaker the resiliency factor of the cane. The reverse is true as well. The resiliency being considered in this instance in a horizontal plane is the strength of the circle, the curvature of the tube of cane.

In other words, the smaller the diameter of the natural curvature of the cane, the greater the natural resiliency in the blades of the reed when the curvature of the cane is forced into a flatter plane in the finished reed at the tip edge. Conversely, if the diameter of the tube of cane is greater or less round, the natural resiliency will be less when the blades and tube are formed.

The linear resiliency factor of the cane lies in the texture of the cane's fiber. The fiber can be soft or hard, loose or tight in texture. Fortunately, both the horizontal and linear resiliency can be controlled by the gouge and trim of the reed. Also valuable are the shape and fulcrum of the reed.

By "fulcrum," Skinner is referring specifically to wire II and the effects that wires I and II have on each other, and how adjustments to the roundness of wires I and II, and the roundness of the tube behind wire II, affect the aperture and blades (Section 1.5). He goes on to explain that **overall, the resiliency factors determine the correct size of the aperture.**

1.4 GOUGES

There are two *basic* types of gouges—*eccentric and concentric*—with many variations among them, as shown in Figure 1.4; see also Figure 6.4 for elliptical and inverted gouges. The blade of a concentric gouger will cut the cane to the same depth all over; the blade of an eccentric gouger, being larger in radius than the original section of cane, will cut away more material at the edges than in the middle.

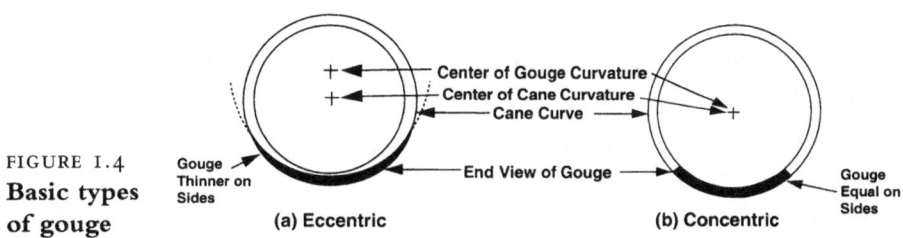

FIGURE 1.4
Basic types of gouge

(a) Eccentric   (b) Concentric

With the eccentric gouge, the greater the eccentricity, the weaker the resiliency factor. In other words, the greater the radius of the scraper blade, the thinner the cane will be in the wings and mid-range areas. Likewise, with the concentric gouge, the thinner the gouge, the weaker the resiliency factor. The reverse is also true for both types. The gouge affects the sound of the reed because it determines the size of the air space inside the reed. The eccentric gouge makes the dimension of the reed smaller inside in width than the concentric gouge. There is consequently less depth in a reed made with the eccentric gouge. The eccentric gouge, however, gives a harder outline (silhouette) to the sound. The lows in a reed made with this gouge lie in a harder texture of the cane fiber due to the gouge being thinner on the sides. The closer to the bark (rind) the fibers are, the harder the texture of the cane.

With the concentric gouge, the lows are in the same texture of the cane as the highs, resulting in a more homogeneous sound.

In other words, the eccentric gouge removes cane from the *inside* of the blades, in the areas associated with mid- and low-range. The remaining fibers in these areas—the fibers in the completed reed—are from closer to the bark and harder (more resilient) than the fibers used in the high range (backbone, or spine). However, with the concentric gouge, in order to make the blades vibrate properly, cane will have to be removed from the mid- and low-range areas from the *outside* of the blades in the profile. Thus, the fibers that the reed uses in these areas are farther from the bark and are softer or less resilient. The concentric gouge provides a *more homogeneous sound* than the eccentric gouge because the fibers on the inside of the blades of the concentric gouge are the same for the low, mid, and high areas, whereas the fibers on the inside of the blades of the eccentric gouge become harder and more resilient as they move from the spine to the edges of the reed. Skinner's reference to a "harder outline (silhouette)" to the eccentrically gouged reed is an aural description of a physical reality: namely, that the reed is made from harder cane along the edges of the blades. The reference to "less depth" with an eccentrically gouged reed is mostly a description of the fact that there tends to be less air space on the inside of the reed, and what that means in terms of how you control the reed on the instrument. Finally, the preferred gouge for the Straight Taper reed (Chapter 3) is the eccentric gouge, and for the Tip Taper reed (Chapter 4) the concentric gouge.

1.5 APERTURE, TRIM, AND VOICING

To further enhance the control of the aperture in a linear plane, we can enhance the linear resiliency with three factors:

a) Fulcrum setting (wire placements and their elevation)
b) Shape (built-in cone, etc.)
c) Inner (linear) enhancement of the gouge and the texture of the tip, and the length of the support. (The simplest version of linear enhancement is the Tip Undercut described at Step 3.8.1: sandpaper is drawn out from the tip edge of the Straight Taper reed, thus sloping or pyramiding the inside of the tip edge toward the upper surface of the blades.)

When wire I is used as the capo d'astro, the fulcrum setting (wire II) must maintain the aperture to be tuned without the help of wire I.

The size of the area of the reed in vibration determines the voicing of the reed by pitch and by the depth of the air chamber over which the area of the reed is in vibration.

At this point, let us discuss the trim's controlling effect upon the resiliency factor of the reed. The trim's effect depends upon where the player places the embouchure on the reed. If the embouchure is placed on the back of the reed near the collar or wire I, then the wings must be longer. This weakens the aperture to the extent that it is sensitive to a much lighter pressure of the embouchure.

If the player is more comfortable with a point of embouchure more toward the tip edge of the reed, the wings should be shorter and the embouchure stronger to maintain pitch. The air pressure, however, will be less than if the embouchure were placed closer to the collar.

If a dark color of sound is wanted, then the embouchure should be placed nearer to the collar and the vibrating surfaces made longer. If a bright color of sound is wanted, with the same embouchure placement, then the vibrating surfaces should be made shorter.

Skinner could have added that the embouchure for a *brighter* sound would be better placed nearer to the tip edge. This concept translates into the two basic reeds described in Chapters 3 and 4.

The Straight Taper reed is *linearly* enhanced with much of the trim taken out on the inside of the gouge, which is preferably eccentric. The characteristic color of such reeds is *bright*,[8] and since the backs of the blades tend to be heavier, the embouchure placement is generally closer to the tip edge.

The Tip Taper reed is *laterally* enhanced by taking cane out of the mid and low areas from the outside of the blades; the gouge is preferably concentric. Since the back part of the reed has primarily parallel fibers and therefore less resiliency, the embouchure can be placed nearer to the collar, the reed is *swallowed*, and the characteristic color is *dark*. Furthermore, if cane has been taken out of the sides of the blades at the back to lower the *natural low pitches* of the reed, this has the effect of increasing the vibrating surfaces and thus making the sound *dark*.

---

8. The terms "bright" and "dark" are difficult to clarify. The author is grateful to Chris Weait for the following suggestion: "'Bright' is more nasal, reedier, . . . 'dark' is less nasal, less reedy." For the author, "dark" is a more covered, dampened timbre with an emphasis on lower overtones, while "bright" is a more open, carrying sound with an emphasis on higher overtones.

CHAPTER 2
ESSENTIAL TOOLS FOR REED MAKING

2.1 SCRAPING WHEELS

Perhaps the single most distinctive aspect of Skinner's teaching and reed making was his development and use of the *scraping wheels* (Figure 2.1). With these tools, Skinner could alter the gouge and customize the inside dimensions of any reed. In a certain sense, his scraping wheels were at the center of his philosophy of **building a world inside a reed**.

His friend and neighbor in Jonesport, Hans Taubenberger,[9] machined the sets of scraping wheels with a handle that Skinner and his students used. Taubenberger made a set of eight wheels out of a cone of steel with the following radii (in inches): 16/32, 20/32, 24/32, 28/32, 32/32, 36/32, 40/32, 48/32. He also made a special 30/32-inch scraping wheel that could not be derived from his original cone. Throughout this book, references to these wheels have maintained Skinner's designations. Scraper #32 means a scraping wheel that is 1 inch (32/32) in diameter, while #24 refers to a scraping wheel 3/4 inch (24/32) in diameter. Otherwise, Skinner rarely used non-metric measurements.

In addition to these wheels, the author had Taubenberger make 56/32 (1-3/4 inch) and 64/32 (2 inch) wheels. Standard sets tended to be a handle and wheels #20 through #48, or a handle and #24 and #32.

2.2 MANDRELS

2.2.1 Pin mandrels

Hans Taubenberger also made *pin mandrels* for Skinner (Figure 2.2). These are used for forming and opening up the tube at wire I, or making it rounder from the inside. There are four pin mandrels:

---

9. The scraping wheels and other specialized tools described in this chapter are available from Custom Cane, Inc. of Pittsburgh, PA (tel. 724-834-6749; e-mail: woodward@westol.com).

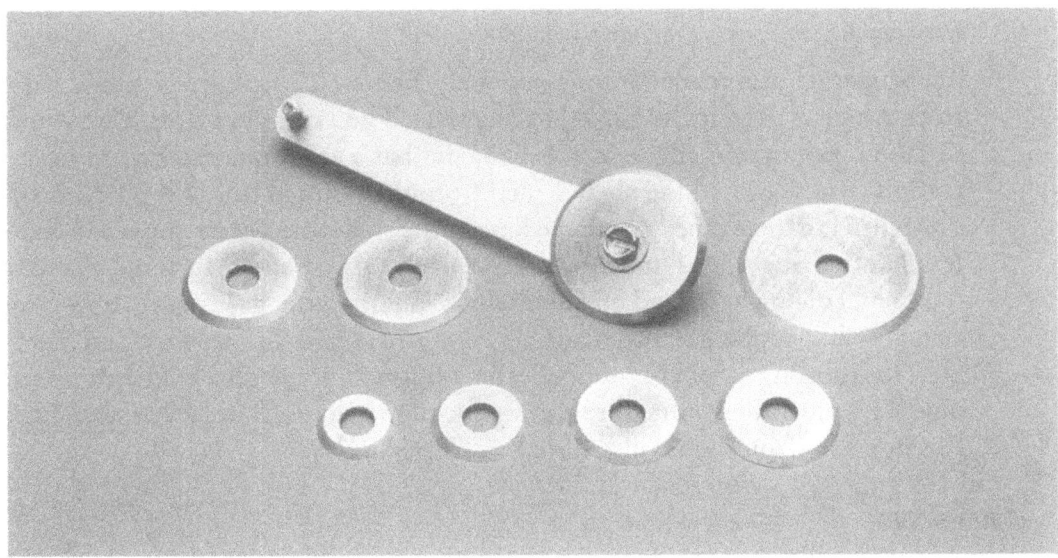

FIGURE 2.1 **Scraping wheels**

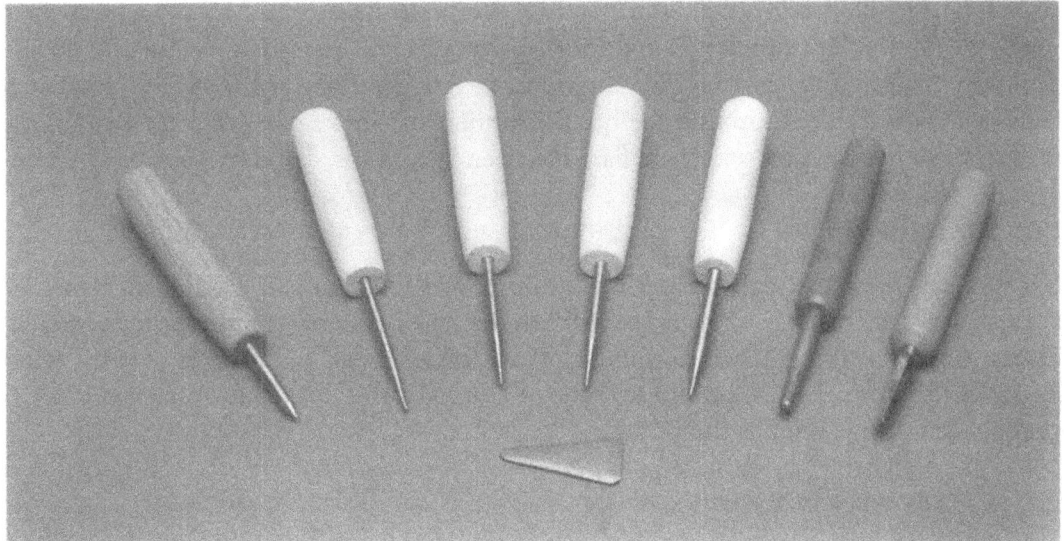

FIGURE 2.2 **Mandrels**

* #9 (9/64 inch in diameter)
* #10 (10/64 inch in diameter)
* #11 (11/64 inch in diameter)
* #13 (13/64 inch in diameter)

Mandrel #9 is the one used normally to open up Straight Taper reeds, where the tube at wire I is more oval; #10 and #11 are used for Tip Taper reeds, where the tube is rounder. Mandrel #13 is normally used for contrabassoon reeds.

2.2.2 *Forming mandrels, contra mandrel, holding mandrel*

Taubenberger also made *forming mandrels*. The 10/12 mandrel is made from stock which is 3/16 inch (12/64) in diameter. The taper goes from 12/64 inch to 10/64 inch over a length of 3/4 inch, and has a short pointed tip. An insert mark is placed around the shaft 1 inch from the pointed tip. The 10/12 mandrel is used to form tubes where the flare of the shape has been removed (Chapters 3 and 4, Steps 3.6.1 and 4.6.1, respectively). The parallel forming mandrel (#11 or 11/64 inch) is used on reeds which maintain the flare in the tube (Section 8.7). Taubenberger also made a #13 *contra mandrel* (13/64 inch in diameter) for forming tubes (Figure 2.9). In addition, Skinner also talked about using a #11 and #10 mandrel for forming the tube with the flare still on the shape (Section 8.7). You should also have a *holding mandrel*.[10]

2.3 REAMERS

For the first reaming, Skinner used a *drill reamer*, consisting of a 3/16-inch drill bit mounted in a handle. The drill is inserted 18 mm (marked by a piece of tape on the shaft), creating a tube. He followed with a slightly conical *file reamer*, inserted 17 mm. Taubenberger made the file reamer from the end of a 3/16-inch rattail file mounted in a handle. In addition, you might also want a *slightly larger reamer* (such as those made by Fox) to ream a "finished" reed if it leaks around the bocal. Skinner also spoke of using a #9 machinist's drill for reaming the tube when the flare has been left on the shape (Section 8.7).

2.4 SHAPER

Skinner had several straight shapers, including Fox #1, #2, and #3, Pisano shapers, and a Prestini Knochenhauer shaper. In addition, he had many brass templates created by disassembling, soaking, flattening, and copying various reeds. These include shapes that had slightly convex blades similar to some of Carl Mechler's reeds. The most common shaper used in this book is the Fox #2 (Figure 2.3).

2.5 KNIVES AND PLAQUES

Skinner recommended having at least three knives. A *regular knife* for post-final trim work should be able to scrape the blades and not chatter. A knife with a heavy spine

---

10. The precise dimensions of the holding mandrel are not critical, as long as the reed, when placed on the mandrel, is relatively secure, and as long as the mandrel does not enlarge the tube or change the wire shapes. The holding mandrel is useful for many tasks, such as holding the reed while you put the wrapping on, and while you work on the blades with a knife. The shaft should be at least 1-1/2 inch (4 cm) long, and the large diameter should be roughly 1/4 inch with a slope to about 5/32 inch at a rounded tip.

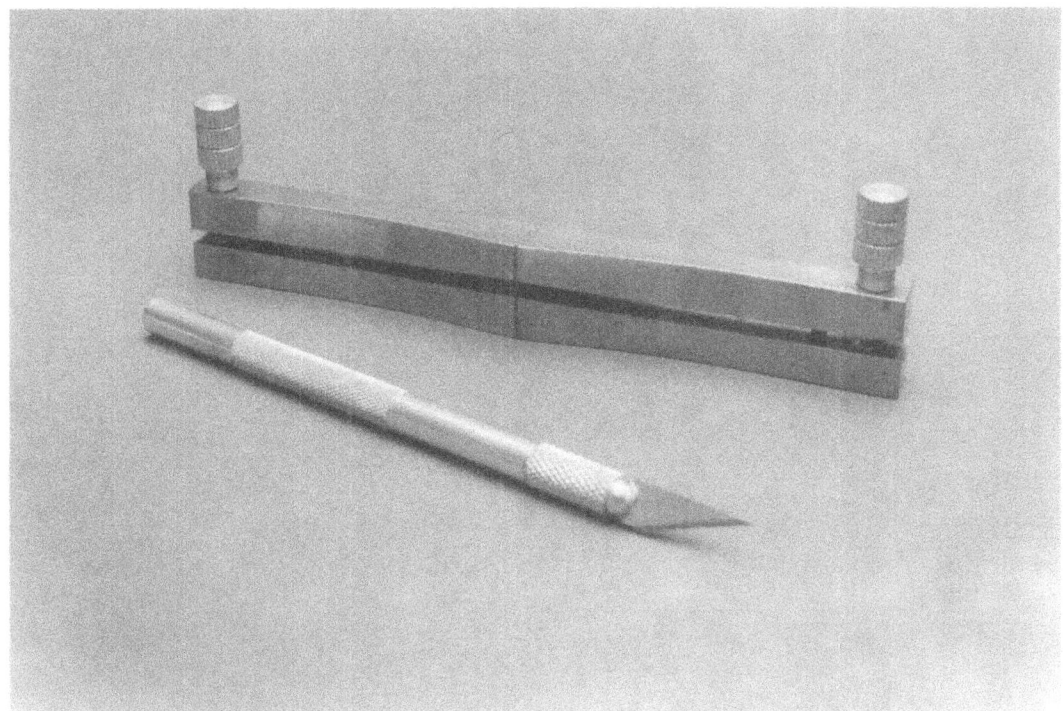

FIGURE 2.3 **Fox #2 straight shaper and Exacto knife with #11 blade**

is required for Parallel-Sides Pre-Trim (Sections 3.5 and 4.5) and hand-profiling. This knife should be heavy enough not to chatter when removing bark. Finally, for shaping, center-panel scoring, and a myriad of other tasks, an *Exacto* knife with *#11 blades* is needed (Figure 2.3).

Plaques, both metal and plastic, are inserted into the aperture of the reed to allow you to work on the tip edge and the blades with knives, files, and sandpaper. They are shaped like arrowheads and are approximately 0.38 mm long and 0.18 mm wide at their widest point. In addition, plaques are convex on both surfaces, matching the aperture of the reed when inserted.

2.6 FILES AND SANDPAPER

Skinner recommended three types of 5-inch Exacto files (or hobby files): *flat bastard*, *knife edge*, and *rattail* (Figure 2.4). The flat bastard is used as an alternative to the knife on the blades. The knife-edge file is used to put wire and collar marks on the cane, and the rattail file is used to clean debris out of the tube. A large flat bastard file is also needed for filing the butt of the tube so that the reeds can stand up on a flat surface (Steps 3.6.16 and 4.6.16). In addition, a sapphire file or *metal emery board* is required for fine work on the blades and for enhancing the tubes (Section 5.3).

16   Chapter 2

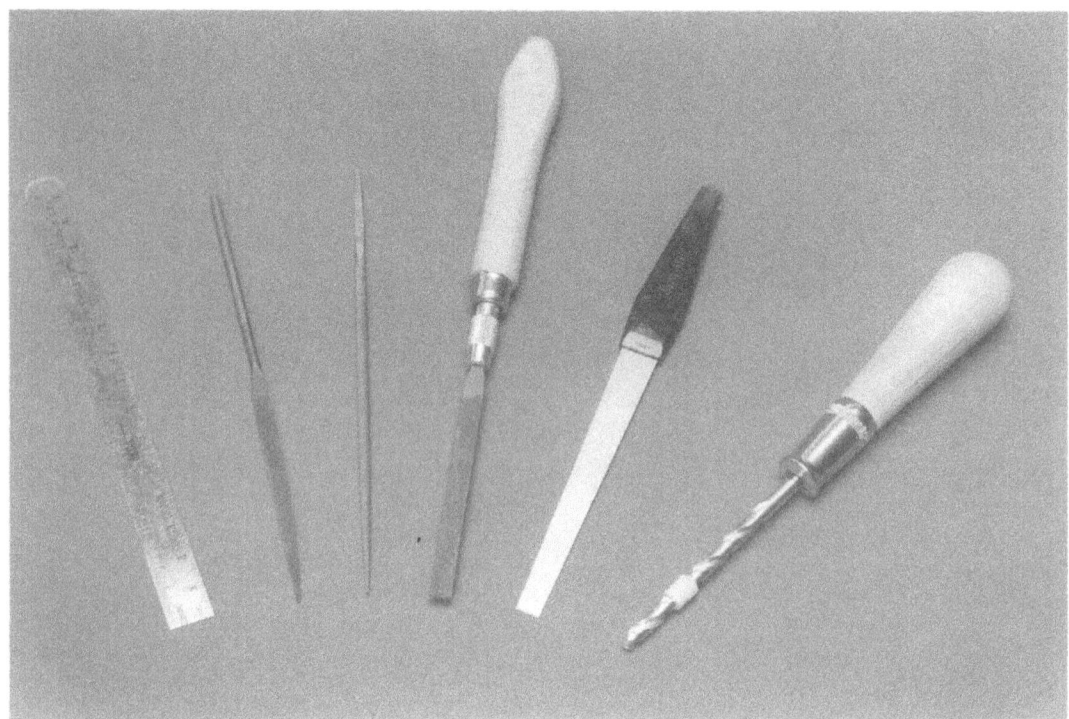

FIGURE 2.4 **Ruler, files, and drill reamer**

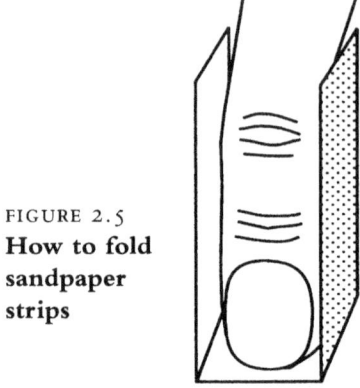

FIGURE 2.5
How to fold sandpaper strips

Skinner required five grades of sandpaper: 120 DRY, 200 DRY, 220 WD (wet or dry), 320 WD, and 400 WD. The "wet or dry" sandpaper is useful when the blades are wet.

When using sandpaper, Skinner recommended that you cut it into strips about 15 mm wide by at least 5 cm long. Make two right-angle folds, and place the tip of your index finger on the sandpaper (Figure 2.5), grasping the sides with your thumb and middle finger. With this procedure, you can control the pressure of the sandpaper on the reed and maintain a relatively good view of what you are doing.

2.7 PLIERS AND END-NIPPER

For wire work, *5-inch pliers* are needed (Figure 2.6), preferably with parallel jaws so that when you change the shapes of wires I and II, the force vectors will be exactly at right angles to the circle or oval of wire. For adjustments to the area between wires II and III, 5-inch parallel-jaw *needle-nose pliers* are also recommended. To clip the tip of the reed, Skinner recommended a pair of 5-inch jeweller's end-nippers. More sophisticated tip clippers are also available.

Essential Tools for Reed Making   17

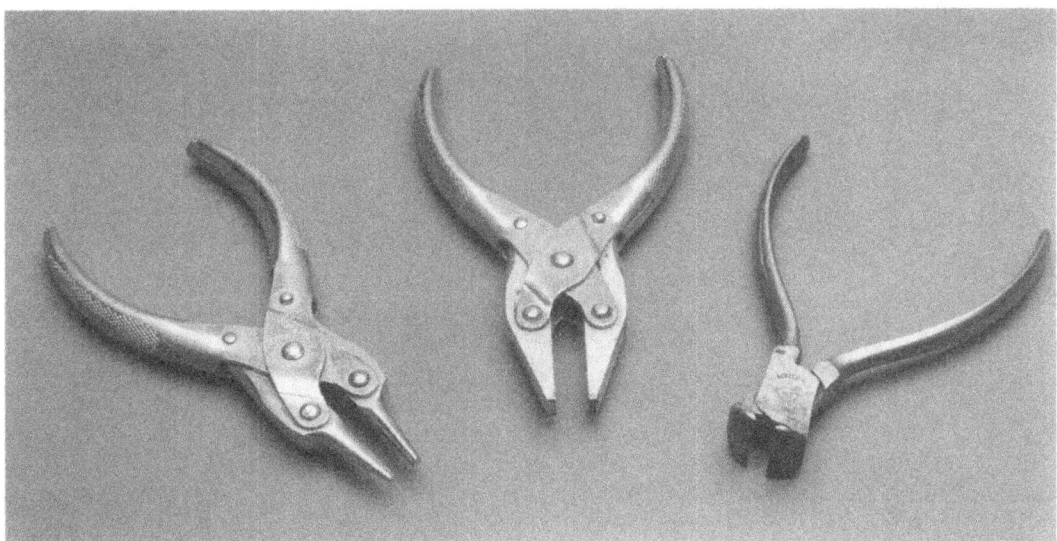

FIGURE 2.6 **Pliers and end-nipper**

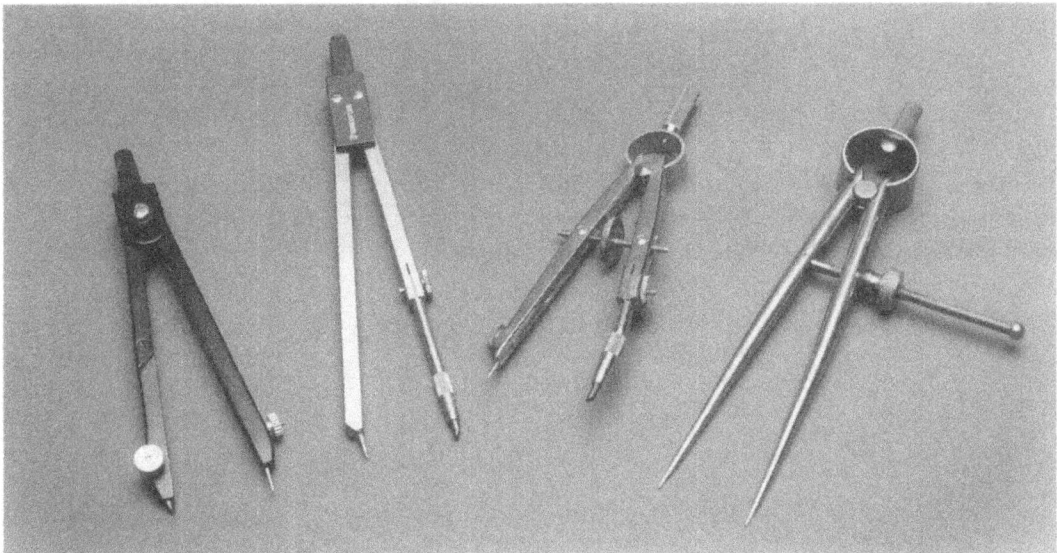

FIGURE 2.7 **Dividers and compasses**

2.8 RULERS, DIVIDERS, AND COMPASSES

A very basic tool is the *metal 15-cm ruler* (6-inch ruler with metric markings). Skinner always had several machine dividers and *pencil compasses* (Figure 2.7). So many measurements are necessary that it makes sense to have dividers and pencil compasses preset to specific lengths. Another useful tool is a *caliper ruler* for outside measurements, specifically the width of the tube at the wire and collar marks.

FIGURE 2.8 *(above)*
Micrometer/dial indicator

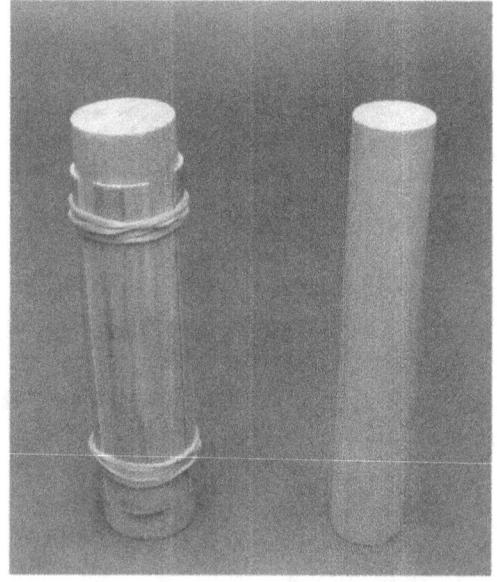

FIGURE 2.9 *(right)*
Doweling dryers

FIGURE 2.10 *(below)*
Contrabassoon reed tools *(from left to right):* **brass template, #13 pin mandrel, 7/32-inch drill reamer, 5/16-inch file reamer, plaque**

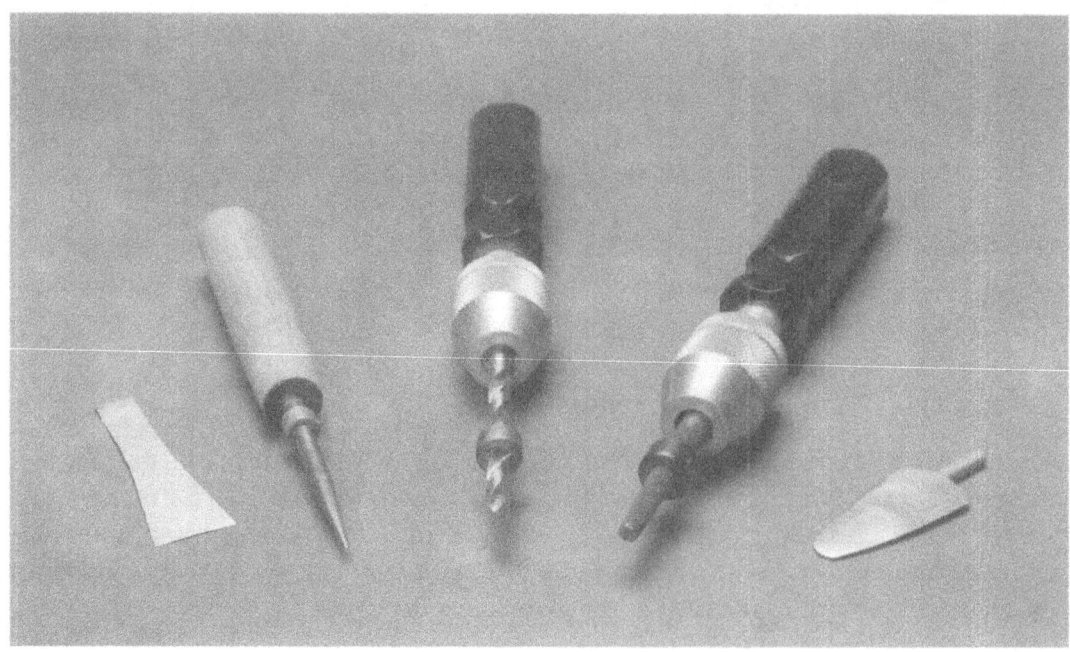

2.9 Wire, String, and Glue

For this book, Skinner specified *22-gauge soft brass wire*. However, many of Skinner's students have said that to them he specified *21 gauge*. Both work perfectly well.

The string that Skinner used in Maine was *blueberry thread*, a ubiquitous string used locally during blueberry season to mark off large sections of blueberry patches. *Cotton crochet thread* is perfectly acceptable.

Skinner always put the first coat of glue on the wrapping with *Duco household cement*. However, any non-toxic, waterproof, fast-drying household cement will do. The final coat of paint was a colored *model-airplane dope*. Fingernail polish can also substitute for the dope.

2.10 Other Tools

A micrometer/dial indicator in metric units is needed to measure the thickness of the blades (Figure 2.8).

Also needed are 6-inch lengths of 1-1/4-inch doweling on which to dry the gouged pieces of cane. Some of Skinner's applications also called for 1-inch doweling dryers, as shown in Figure 2.9.

The *easel* used for working on the piece of cane before folding is a dowel 1 inch in diameter and 12 inches long.[11] A piece of opaque Plexiglas that is 1 inch in diameter can also be used as an easel. The advantage of the Plexiglas is that the cane can be examined with back-lighting without removing it from the easel. Finally, a *desk lamp* is necessary to allow examination of the cane and reeds with back lighting. Figure 2.10 shows the tools used for contrabassoon-reed making (Chapter 10).

---

11. The author uses a 1-1/4-inch-diameter dowel easel because his gouged cane has been "double sunk" and dried on 1-1/4 dowels.

CHAPTER 3[12]

THE STRAIGHT TAPER REED: LOU SKINNER'S INTERPRETATION OF CARL MECHLER'S REED

3.1 PREPARATION OF TUBES, GOUGING, AND PROFILING

3.1.1 Split cane longitudinally into four parts

The tube of cane should be about 150 mm long, straight, and 24 to 26 mm in outside diameter. Split the cane lengthwise by pressing downward onto the end of the tube with a heavy knife while the tube is vertical to the bench. Split the cane first in half and then into quarters. If the cane is less than 24 mm in outside diameter, split it into three parts only.

3.1.2 Soak cane (the Sink Method)

In a large jar with a lid, soak the cane until it sinks (about five days). Change the water each day and keep the cane covered. Besides softening the cane, soaking leaches out some of the sap and impurities. After five days, the water should remain clear. Drain the water and leave the cane in the covered jar for two more days.

---

12. Chapters 3 and 4, dealing with the construction of the two basic reeds, were written in preliminary form by the author and approved by Skinner in 1988. They formed the basis for the handouts at the lecture given by the author, Bill Woodward, and Gerry Corey at the 1994 IDRS conference, and did not include the Sink Method. However, after finishing the first draft of the book, the author, in reviewing his notes and tapes from the summer of 1990, realized that Skinner had wanted to include the Sink Method as an alternative to the Windsor Mill Process. Therefore, as a compromise, Step 3.1.2 was replaced with the Sink Method in Chapter 3. The same step in Chapter 4 was kept the way it had been approved in 1988 and presented in 1994. The reader can choose which method to use; both methods will work for both reeds.

3.1.3 *Cut cane to length for gouging machine*

Cut the cane to 120 mm, or 1 mm shorter than the gouger bed.

3.1.4 *Cut off sharp edges (fillier)*

Holding one end of the piece of cane, cut the edges off each side, producing flats on each edge of the inside of the tube. Reverse the cane and repeat on the other end, so that the flats are consistent across the entire length of the cane. The cane should then fit in the gouger with the flats aligned with the top surface of the gouger bed.

3.1.5 *Gouge cane*

Gouge the cane while it is wet. The gouge should be eccentric, approximately 1.25 mm (±0.05 mm) in thickness in the center and 0.80 mm at the sides. If the cane is hard, use a thicker gouge (1.35 mm to 1.40 mm) and follow up with a deeper profile, since the softer part of the cane will be farther from the bark. Gouge the cane in both directions to compensate for lack of symmetry in the tubes.

NOTE: When ordering pre-gouged cane, request pieces 120 mm in length with an eccentric gouge 1.25 mm to 1.30 mm in the middle and a minimum of 0.80 mm at the edges.

3.1.5.a *Dry cane on 1-1/4-inch doweling for two to three days*

Attach four or five pieces of cane with elastic bands to 6-inch pieces of 1-1/4-inch hardwood doweling and dry for two or three days. Wet cane is dark, but dry cane is yellow; green cane can be used successfully with the *Sink Method*.

3.1.5.b *Soak cane for two or three more days and dry on doweling for two or three more days*

Skinner stated that **this double-soaking method produces cane in which the grain will not rise up when soaked later.** Skinner suspected that Del Negro gouged his cane similarly. **Del said his gouge was smooth because he sandpapered it. However, when soaked, the grain didn't rise. If you soak the cane 24 hours, gouge it and sand it, the grain will rise when the cane is soaked again.**

3.1.6 *Profile cane (with profiling machine)*

There are two methods of removing the bark between the collar marks: *profiling by machine* and *profiling by hand*. The machine method is outlined here; hand-profiling is outlined in Chapter 4 (Step 4.1.6.b).

a) The cane should be profiled by machine while it is still wet. If the cane is dry, soak it for 2 hours in warm water before profiling. For a Straight-Taper reed, the profiler should be set to produce the thicknesses described in Figure 3.1.

22   Chapter 3

> NOTE: These measurements are for *dry* cane. Wet cane is approximately 0.03 mm thicker. Since the gouge is eccentric, it is not necessary to profile from side to side.[13]

b) Smooth entire blade with 220 WD and finish with 400 WD.

c) Add centerfold mark on the convex surface of the cane at 60 mm and gently score across the cane with a knife-edge file.

NOTE: The vital *final measurements on dry cane* are approximately 0.90 mm in thickness at the collar (30 mm from the butt end), 0.68 mm in thickness at the 43-mm mark from the butt (half-way down the blade), and 0.55 mm in thickness at the 50-mm mark from the butt. The thickness at 50 mm should never be less than 0.50 mm. Since more cane will be taken out at the Parallel-Sides Pre-Trim (Section 3.5), the cane at this profiled stage, measuring along the spine, can therefore be approximately 0.05 mm thicker—0.95 mm at the 30-mm mark, 0.73 mm at the 43-mm mark, 0.61 mm at 50-mm mark, and 0.45 mm at the 60-mm mark (the center). The Tip Taper profile described by Figure 3.1 is achieved by using a double-sloping template or guide on the profiling machine. You can also add the Tip Taper to a heavier Straight Taper profile with another machine (Step 4.1.6.a). The critical factor is that the Tip Taper profile, whether achieved by a double-sloping template or by a second machine, should be a maximum of 0.80 mm thick or a minimum of 0.65 mm thick at the 50-mm mark.

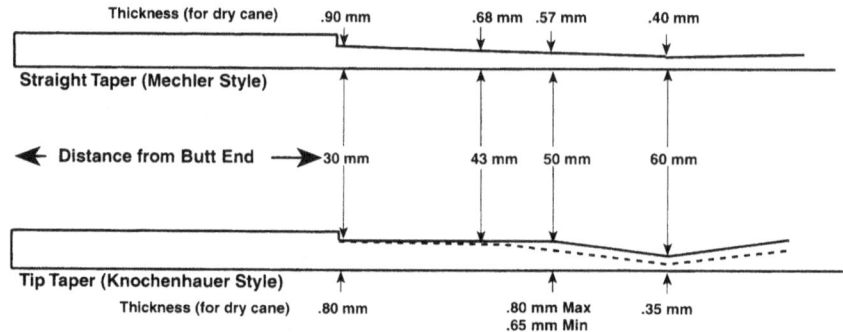

FIGURE 3.1 **Side view of Straight and Tip Taper Profiles on dry cane**

3.1.7   Tie profiled cane to a piece of doweling

Tie profiled cane to a piece of doweling 3.175 cm (1-1/4 inch) in diameter and let dry. The cane takes 12 hours to dry at room temperature, 6 hours in a warming

---

13. Side-to-side profiling refers to cane being removed more on the sides than in the center. On a Pfeifer profiler, this is done by having a flat center on the axel of the easel. For eccentrically gouged cane, Skinner insisted that the axel be turned so that it was always rounded on the support, thus producing no side-to-side variation in thickness.

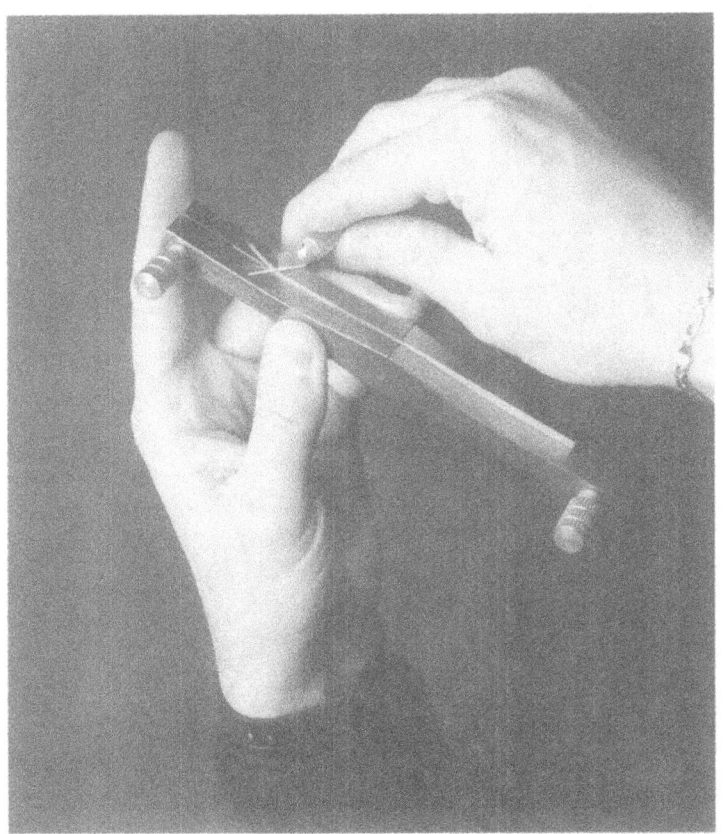

FIGURE 3.2
Cane being shaped

oven or a gas oven with a pilot light, or 20 minutes directly under a 60-watt lamp. Using wet cane for the next steps is inadvisable, since drying causes shrinkage, making the measurements inaccurate.

3.2 PRE-TRIM

The inside of the gouge of the cane is critical both in the tube and blade areas. Alteration to the gouge—and consequently variations to the reed style—can take place at this point. The reed described here, however, has no alteration to the gouge if the Windsor Mill Process (Section 3.3) is left out.

3.2.1 *Smooth and polish inside of gouge with 400 WD sandpaper; leave the dust, and polish with the smooth paper side of the sandpaper.*

3.2.2 *Shape cane*[14]

For this style of reed, use a Fox #2 straight shaper, Prestini Knochenhauer, or Pisano #2. Before placing the cane in the shaper, ensure that the piece is cut

---

14. Another shaping technique that uses a masking-tape template is described in Section 10.2.

FIGURE 3.3
Feathered blades and butt end

to 120 mm so that it will fit between the internal pins. Next, center the cane according to the gouge. For example, if the machine profile is slightly off center, the cane can be offset slightly to one side in the shaper to correct for the gouge. Make sure the centerfold line of the reed matches the center mark on the shaper.

Use a sharp Exacto knife (#11 blade) to shape the cane (Figure 3.2). Hold the shaper in the left hand with one edge up, making sure your left hand is below the surface of the shaper (left-handed people, of course, use opposite hands). Hold the Exacto knife in a fist in your right hand (the fist will prevent the blade from stabbing you as you draw it toward yourself). Begin by placing the blade just beyond the center point of the edge of the quadrant nearest to you. Pull the blade toward you, cutting a slice 2 mm to 3 mm thick. Stop cutting at the narrowest point on the shaper—do not cut all the way to the butt. This will allow you to copy the flair of the shaper onto the butt of the reed—and will keep you from cutting away a portion of the side of the tube from under the shaper at the butt. Continue to *feather* the cane back to the narrowest part of the shaper, cutting closer to the side of the shaper with every stroke.

When your Exacto knife has reached the shaper from the center point to the narrowest point, turn the shaper around so that the quadrant you have just worked on is farthest from you. *Feather* the cane away in the same fashion at the butt end (Figure 3.3).

Reverse the shaper several times as needed to ensure that the piece of cane cut out is removed from the shaper without causing a nick anywhere along the shape. (A nick or split on a fiber in the blade area will generally render the reed useless, while a nick on the tube could cause leaking.)

Turn the shaper over and work on the opposite quadrant. Then, repeat for the other two quadrants, at the other end of the shaper.

3.2.3 Mark collar and wire positions

With a pair of machine dividers, mark on the bark the positions of wire II, wire

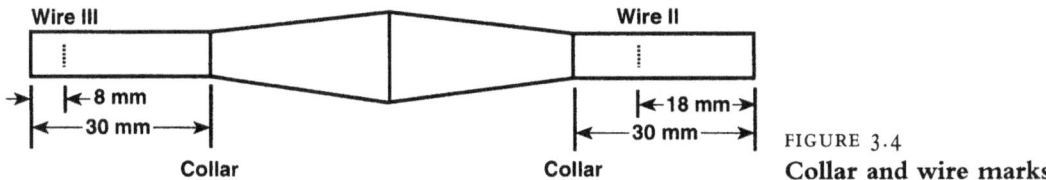

FIGURE 3.4
Collar and wire marks

III, and the collar, as shown in Figure 3.4, always measuring from the butt end. If necessary, enlarge the marks with a knife-edge file.

3.3 ENHANCEMENT OF THE INSIDE OF THE TUBE (WINDSOR MILL PROCESS)[15]

The process described here, the Windsor Mill Process, was originally taught by Skinner as an alternative to the Sink Method. Since the Sink Method is described in this chapter, the Windsor Mill Process can be considered a variation (Step 5.1.1 for the original version) and can be left out entirely. However, since Skinner taught the process to so many students in the 1970s and 1980s, a modified version (approved by Skinner) is included here.

Basically, both the Sink Method and the Windsor Mill Process were designed to allow the tube to be formed with a minimum of cracking in the surface of the bark, and to prevent cracks from running into the blades. The Sink Method soaks the cane to make it more malleable, while the Windsor Mill Process removes cane from the inside of the tube. Once the thickness of the cane has been reduced, the tube can be forced around the inserted forming mandrel without creating a serious risk of splitting. Because a layer

---

15. This portion of the process has been slightly altered from the 1994 IDRS handout.

of cane has been removed from the inside of the tube, there is a decrease in pressure on the inside fibers, which decreases the tendency of the outer surface of the tube to split. Furthermore, when cane has been removed from the inside surface of the tube, the fibers on the inner surface of the blades are disconnected at the tube, allowing the blades to vibrate more freely, especially in the lower frequencies. For this reason, the author and Skinner decided to keep the modified Windsor Mill Process in Chapters 3 and 4. The *modification* is that the enhancement procedure here removes half as much cane, or 0.10 mm, as the *original* procedure, which cuts away 0.20 mm of cane (Step 5.1.1).

3.3.1 *With pencil compass, mark the inside of gouge 32 mm from butt end*

3.3.2 *Pilot cut*

Measure the thickness of each butt and decrease this by 0.10 mm. (If the butt is less than 1.20 mm thick, do not make it any thinner than 1.10 mm.) Place the cane on a scraping board (a piece of cardboard tacked to a piece of wood) and scrape a pilot cut down the center, from the 32-mm mark to the butt, with the smallest scraper you have (#24, #20, or #16). Each stroke will remove approximately 0.01 mm, so count strokes and measure frequently (Figure 3.5).

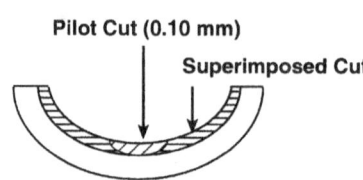

FIGURE 3.5
Cross-section of tube showing pilot and superimposed cuts

3.3.3 *Superimposed cut*

With a pencil, draw a sawtooth line from the 32-mm mark to the butt, as shown in Figure 3.6. Superimpose scraper #32 onto the original pilot cut, scraping from the 32-mm mark to off the butt end, until pencil marks are removed (Figure 3.5).

3.3.4 *Sand entire inside butt with 200 DRY and 400 WD*

Smooth out the transition from the Windsor Mill enhancement slightly into the blades.

3.3.5 *Define collar of reed*

When you are using machine-profiled cane, you will need to remove the burr between the collar and the blade. Place the cane on the easel and score the collar mark (30 mm from the butt) across the tube with a knife-edge file. *Do not chip out the burr yet!*

3.4 CENTER-PANEL SCORING

This procedure is preferred but not required if you use the Sink Method, in which case you can proceed to 3.5. See Figure 3.7 for the score marks described below.

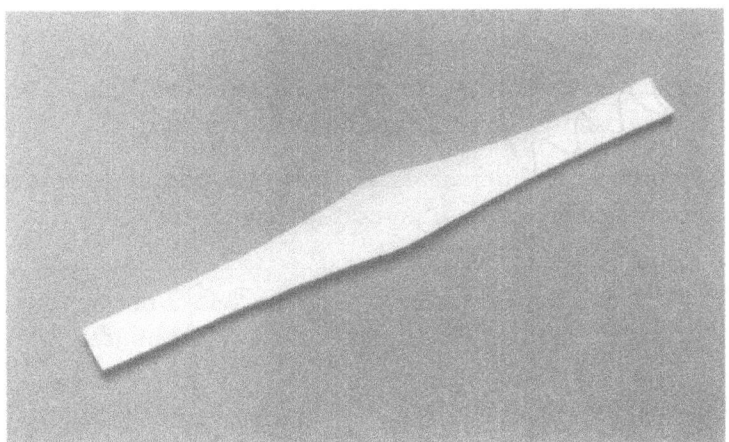

FIGURE 3.6
Sawtooth line on inside of tube

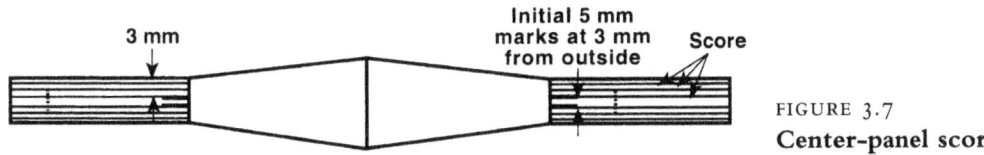

FIGURE 3.7
Center-panel scoring

a) With machine dividers, put a short mark approximately 5 mm long on the bark of the tube, parallel to the sides, inset 3 mm from each side, and running from the collar mark toward the butt, as in Figure 3.7.

b) Score the cane along each 3-mm mark to the butt end. To do this, use the tip of an Exacto knife to penetrate the bark lightly in a line running down and past the butt at right angles to the collar. This is most easily accomplished if you place the cane on the easel and the easel on the table.

c) Score two more lines, parallel to the first, between the edge of the cane and each 3-mm score line.

d) In the final 1 mm at the butt end of each score line, press the Exacto blade right through the cane. It is essential that the score lines all have the same depth and run parallel. The scoring need be only deep enough to penetrate the bark (about 0.20 mm). If the score marks are not parallel and even in depth, the tube will form unevenly when the mandrel is inserted (Step 3.6.5), causing pressure ridges and ruining the balance in the blades. The tube could even split into the blades, causing an irreparable air leak.

e) Chip out the burr of bark in front of the collar; use an Exacto knife, with the cane on the easel. Be careful to continue the thickness of the profile of the blades into the collar. Do not allow the cane to become gradually thicker or thinner at this point by sloping up or down to the collar. Smooth out the area in front of collar with a sapphire file.

3.5 PARALLEL-SIDES PRE-TRIM

This portion of the method is the final and most critical stage of profiling. The blades of the reed are prepared so that they will vibrate freely as a blank as soon as the tip is cut.

NOTE: The following measurements are *minimum thicknesses* of the spine of the blades when the parallel-sides pre-trim is finished (measurements on dry cane):

at collar	0.95 to 0.85 mm thick (measure collar thickness 2 mm in front of collar if the Windsor Mill enhancement has been used)
at 43 mm	0.73 to 0.68 mm thick
at 50 mm	0.62 to 0.56 mm thick
at 60 mm (center)	0.45 to 0.40 mm thick

3.5.1 Mark blades and decrease thickness of profile

   a) With a pencil compass, mark 43 mm and 50 mm (from butt ends) on the top and underside of each blade.

   b) Using a heavy knife with the blade at right angles to the surface of the cane, reduce the thickness of the center portion of the profile, from the collar to the 43-mm mark. When you have finished, the blades should be 0.90 mm thick at 2 mm in front of the collar, and 0.70 mm thick at the 43-mm mark.

   c) If the cane appears to be exceptionally brittle, make the whole blade thinner by another 0.03 mm.

3.5.2 Decrease thickness of blade sides by one-half to no thinner than 0.40 mm at edge

   a) Set pencil compass to 3 mm and mark along blades from collar to reed tip, as shown in Figure 3.8.

   b) Determine the thickness of the side of the blades.

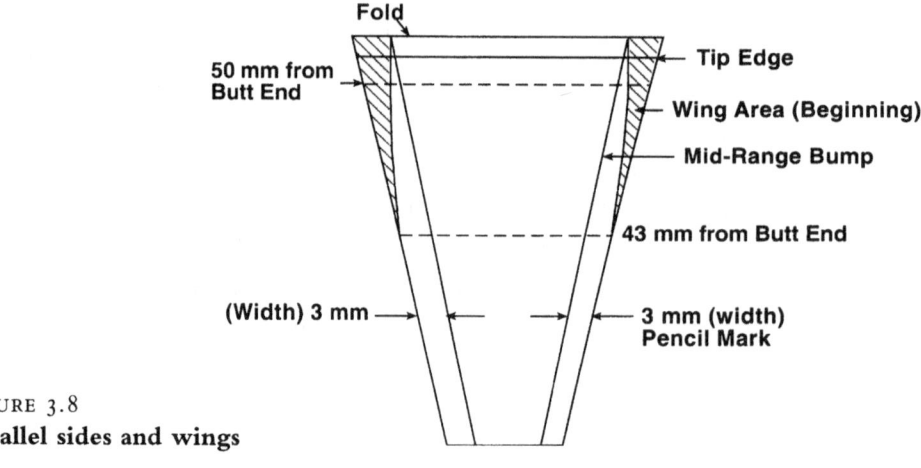

FIGURE 3.8
Parallel sides and wings

c) With the cane on the easel, hold the heavy knife vertically to the cane and pull from the collar to the 50-mm mark parallel to the sides of the shape. Make strokes in one direction only, from the collar to the 50-mm mark, and count the number of strokes (approximately 10) so that you can use the same number of strokes on the other three quadrants. The sides of the blades should be approximately 0.40 mm thick and should slope upward to the 3-mm mark parallel to the shape. Use more strokes on each quadrant if needed. Make sure that the thickness of the cane at the 50-mm mark of the blade, halfway between the center and the edge, does not drop below 0.50 mm.

3.5.3 Remove mid-range bump

Because of Step 3.5.2, you can now see a ridge along roughly the 3-mm mark which parallels the shape. The ridge is removed by gently pulling the knife from the collar to the 50-mm mark, this time parallel with the fibers and not parallel to the sides of the shape. This procedure also begins to establish the wing area. Again, pull only from the collar to the 50-mm mark.

NOTE: The tip edge and wing area do not require much thinning at all.

3.5.4 Pre-trim

Proceed as shown in Figure 3.9, *Pre-trim beginning*.

a) With the cane on the easel, pull the heavy knife from the collar to the fold and back, starting the first stroke at line 1, as indicated in Figure 3.9 (approximately 3 mm in from the edge), and proceeding toward the side, stroke to line 8.

b) Retrace the eight strokes and proceed with three more, closer to the center line (-1, -2, -3).

c) Repeat for each quadrant.

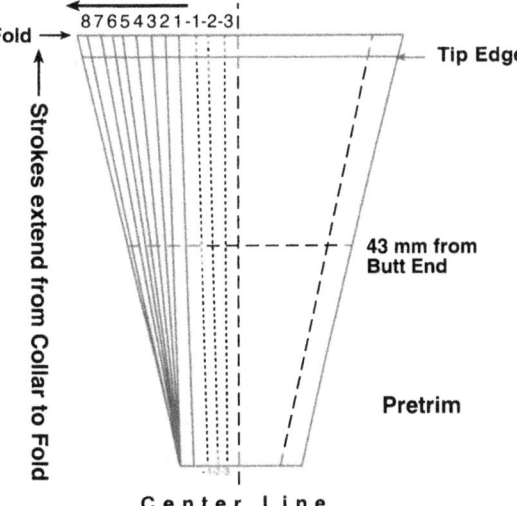

FIGURE 3.9 **Pre-trim beginning**

3.5.5 Sand entire surface lightly with 120 DRY

This sanding will smooth out surfaces that were made uneven by knife work, and will establish a gentle curvature from the center line to the sides.

3.5.6 Establish wings

On each blade, re-mark 43 mm (from the butt end) with a pencil compass, as in Figure 3.10. Using 120 DRY, sand the wing areas, making the sides from the 43 mm mark to fold into a knife edge. However, be careful not to make the edges so thin that the sides disappear. In addition, checking the cane in the light, you should begin to establish the tongue by blending the wings into the center of the tip area.

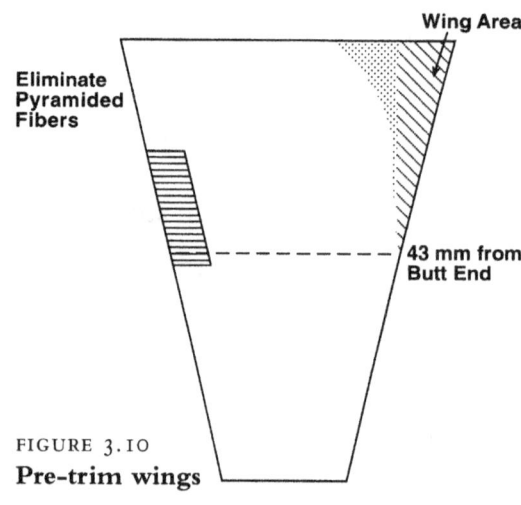

FIGURE 3.10
Pre-trim wings

NOTE: The tendency is to take out too much cane at this stage!

3.5.7 Eliminate pyramided fibers

Using the heavy knife, smooth down the pyramided fibers just in front of the 43-mm mark (Figure 3.10). Pyramided fibers, or a sudden thickness of the cane at this point, will prevent the low pitches from responding.

3.5.8 Sand pyramided fibers

Use 120 DRY to remove bumps from knife work and sand overall with 220 WD.

3.5.9 Re-establish fold line with knife-edge file

3.5.10 Soak cane for 10 to 12 hours or until it sinks

3.6 FORMING AND DRYING[16]

3.6.1 Fold and remove flare

Grasp the reed (with thumbs underneath and forefingers on top, equidistant on each side of the centerfold); fold reed with concave sides inward. If necessary, roll the fold so that the collars are lined up. While holding the two halves

---

16. For a method of forming and drying that does not remove the flare, see Section 8.7. Also, for a discussion on beveling (which is not required on reeds where the flare has been removed), see Section 5.5. This book implies that a single reed is made from the beginning to end by itself. Skinner, of course, had cane and reeds at several stages simultaneously. To keep the cane and string soaked, and to heat the mandrel (3.6.1. to 3.6.15), and to soak the reed (3.8.4), he used a hot pot with a thermostat set to keep the water at approximately 90°C/194°F.

of the reed together, remove the flare from the tube with the Exacto knife so that the sides of the tube are parallel. (On the Fox and Knochenhauer shapes, the tube flares outward from the narrowest point at the wire II mark to the butt. This step removes that flare.)

NOTE: Beveling can be added here, even with the flare removed (Section 5.5 *Beveling Variation*). However, Skinner did not include beveling at this point when working on the book.

3.6.2 *Side-slip top blade to left at butt by about 1 to 2 mm; pinch tip edge of reed*

While holding the reed so that the butt is pointing toward your body, and the tip edge is pointing away, side-slip the butt of the top blade to the left by about 1 to 2 mm. This procedure allows the halves of the tube and the blades to fit together better because one side of the tube will be slightly buried inside the other. The effect of the 1 to 2 mm side-slip will be lessened when the forming mandrel is inserted and turned clockwise.

3.6.3 *Wrap reed, starting at collar and proceeding to 2 mm from butt end; finish with slipknot*

This wrapping is essential so that the tube of the reed will be formed evenly. Use the same cotton crochet thread that will be used to finish wrapping the reed. Begin by laying the standing end of the thread on the upper side of the tube at the collar and wrapping two courses or revolutions over it. This should secure the thread. Continue wrapping carefully and tightly toward the butt end, making sure each course is laid evenly beside the previous course. Do not allow any course to override a neighboring course. Finish with a slipknot.

3.6.4 *Place reed in hot water (90°C/194°F) for 20 minutes*

Heat the 10/12 mandrel in the water for the last 30 seconds.

3.6.5 *Insert the forming mandrel*

Place the 10/12 mandrel into the aperture of the butt end slowly but firmly, up to the mark, gently twisting the mandrel clockwise as needed. Begin by grasping the reed on the sides of the wire III mark with thumb and forefinger. Start pushing the mandrel in gently at first. Make sure that the mandrel goes in straight and not at an angle. Pushing the mandrel in at an angle could cause one side of the tube to arch and crack more than the other. A certain amount of cracking is almost inevitable in the tube (Section 3.4 on *Central Panel Scoring*). The cracking may extend into the blade, but as long as the crack remains on the surface of the cane and does not go right through, the reed is salvageable. Any pressure ridges that are created because of a crack in the surface of the tube must be taken care of in the final trim by removing cane from the blade (with a sapphire file) at the point in the collar where the split enters the blade.

32   Chapter 3

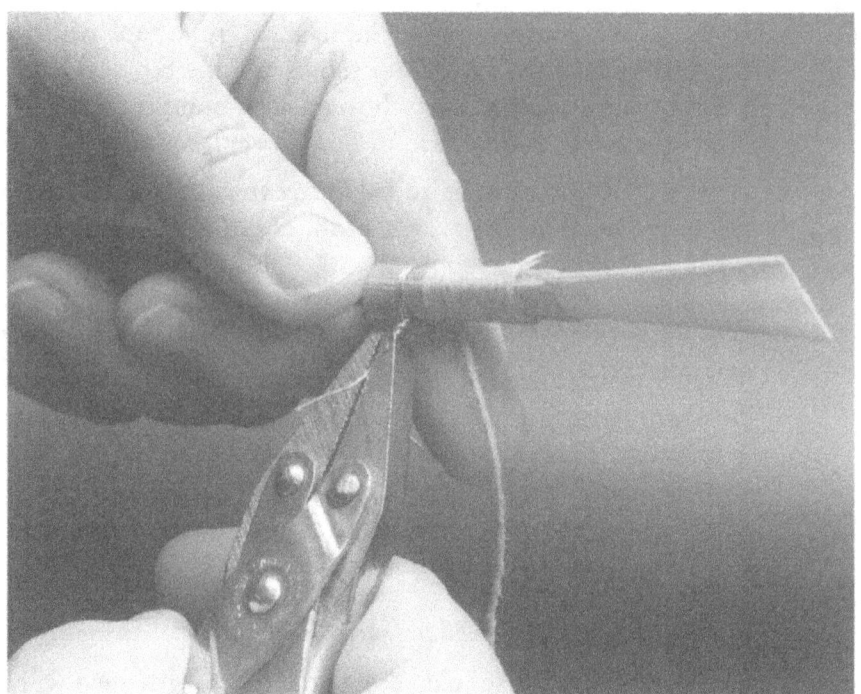

FIGURE 3.11 **Partially unwrapping string and putting on wire III**

3.6.6 Partially unwrap string from butt end to just beyond wire III mark; put on wire III

Pull the string counterclockwise to maintain the tension of the slipknot. Wrap the wire counterclockwise two full turns,[17] making sure that the courses are adjacent and not overlapping.

With your fingers, twist both ends of the wire counterclockwise one or two full turns (Figure 3.11). Tighten with pliers by pulling the twisted wire away from the tube and twisting counterclockwise to snug; four or five full twists should be sufficient. Always pull to tighten and twist to snug. Clip off excess wire above four or five turns.

3.6.7 Remove string and soak string in water

Soak the cotton string first: later, when the string has been put back on the reed and dries, it will shrink tightly around the tube, helping to make a well-formed airtight tube.

---

17. Skinner considered a "full turn" to be one complete revolution of the wires accomplished with the fingers. A "full twist" is a 1/4 turn, using pliers. A "half twist" is therefore 1/8 of a turn, using pliers.

3.6.8 With machine dividers, mark full fundamental length, the distance from wire II mark to tip edge, on the blade at 38 mm

3.6.9 Put on wire II

Follow the same procedures as given in Step 3.6.6, but make sure that the twist of wire II is on the opposite side of the tube from wire III. Pull to tighten, twist (counterclockwise) to lock. Make sure that the tip-edge side of wire II is at the mark. Since the vibrations begin at the tip edge of the reed, wires will affect vibrations beginning on the side of the wire closest to the tip. Therefore, measurements for the bahn length refer to the distance from the tip edge of the cane to the leading edge of wire I.

3.6.10 Butt molding

With parallel-jaw pliers, gently mold the butt all the way around the mandrel from wire III to off the end.

3.6.11 Center-panel molding

Gently mold the center of the tube, not the sides, between wires II and III around the mandrel with parallel jaw pliers.

3.6.12 Retighten wires II and III and remove overlap on outside edge of cane between wire II and collar

The overlap on the edge of the cane is removed (with an Exacto knife) to make sure that wire I, when it is put on, will conform as closely as possible to the tube, as in Figure 3.12.

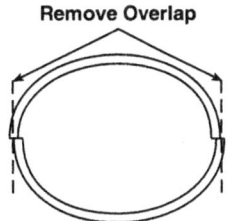

FIGURE 3.12
Cross-section of tube at wire I, showing removal of overlap

3.6.13 Narrow the tip edge to 15 mm if needed

This step can be accomplished by filing gently with a sapphire file from the collar to the tip on the sides of the shape. Use the coarse or fine side of the sapphire file, depending on how much cane has to be removed. The tip edge (marked as Full Fundamental Length) should be no less than 15 mm wide. If a flatter pitch is desired, the tip edge should be left at 15.5 mm at this stage; the reed can be narrowed later.

3.6.14 With knife-edge file, cut in adjustment notches (four or five) between wires II and III on center and sides of tube

Adjustment notches (Figure 3.13) are essential for later alterations to the tube between wires II and III, which will affect response and pitch.

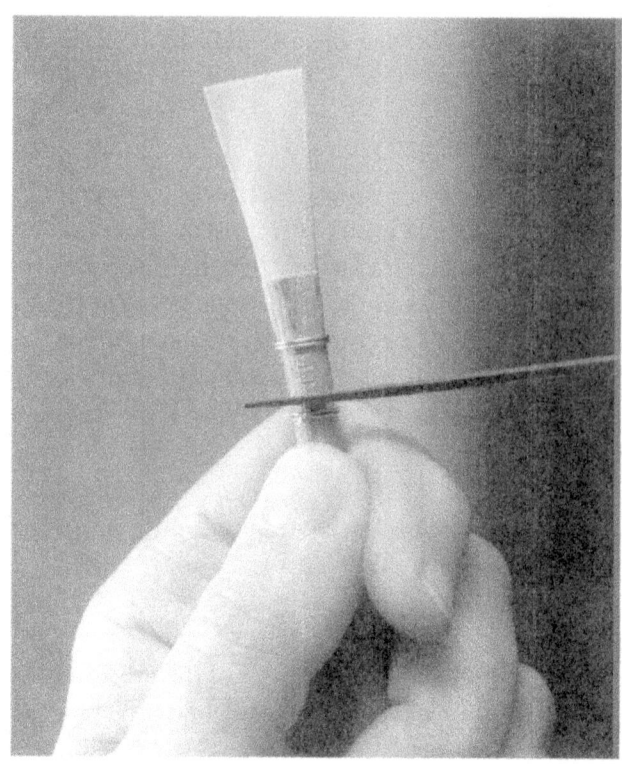

FIGURE 3.13
Adjustment notches

3.6.15 While reed and string are wet, put binding on reed[18]

3.6.16 File butt end of reed flat so reed can stand vertically

3.6.17 Ream reed with drill and file reamers

    Push the drill reamer in, twisting clockwise to 18 mm (wire II). The file reamer is inserted to 17 mm, twisting counterclockwise. Use of these tools can be facilitated by putting tape on the shafts to mark the depth measurements.

18. Most bassoonists put a wrapping of string over wire III, sometimes referred to as a "turk's head." There are almost as many variations of this wrapping as there are reed makers. The purpose of the wrapping is to allow the player to grasp the reed and, to a lesser extent, to keep the reed intact. Placing the reed on a holding mandrel, the author begins by looping the cotton string onto the upturned twist of wire III. The string is then pulled tightly and laid beside the blade side of wire III for 1-1/4 revolutions. The string is then crossed diagonally over wire III to the butt side. A string is laid down for a half-revolution beside wire III and is then brought diagonally back to the blade side for another half-revolution. When the first diagonal cross-over is reached, the string is laid just beyond and beside (not on top of) this cross-over, and returned to the butt side of wire III. The author continues this process until wire III is no longer visible. At this point, 2 complete revolutions of string are made around the tube on the butt side of the wrapping. A third revolution overlaps the 2 and returns the string to the ball for the last diagonal cross-over. The last diagonal cross-over on the blade side begins a single layer of tightly wrapped string around the reed tube, filling in the space

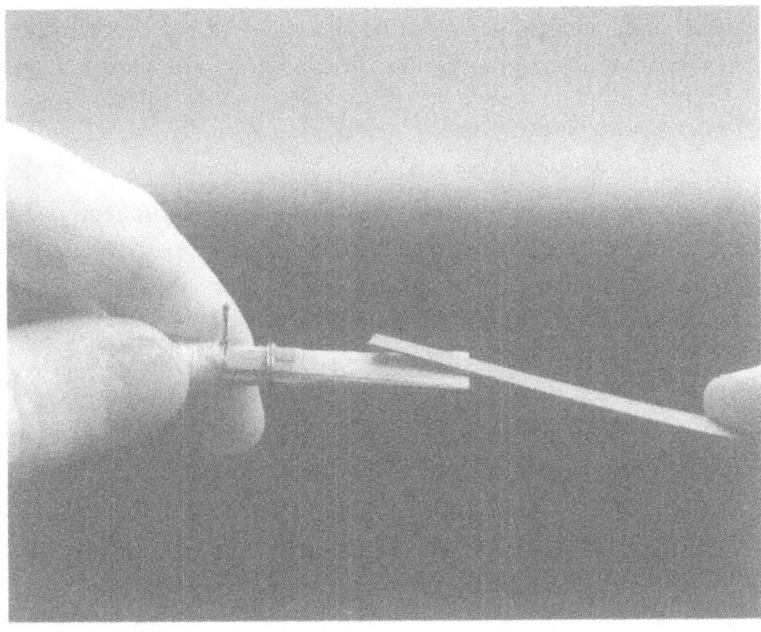

FIGURE 3.14
Sapphire file on tip edge

3.6.18 Straighten sides

If the sides of the shape have twisted apart as a result of reaming, realign them by twisting wire III with the forming mandrel in, or by straightening the sides again with a sapphire file.

3.6.19 Cut reed

This can be done with a knife and cutting block, with a pair of 5-inch jeweller's end-nippers, or with a tip cutter. Cut reed at Full Fundamental Length: 38 mm from wire II, or 56 mm from the butt.

3.6.20 Adjust side-slipping

To ensure that the reed does not leak, adjust the side-slipping of the blades so that the upper right side is slightly inside the lower right when viewed from the butt end. The tip is not side-slipped.

3.6.21 Clip corners of reed

The angle should be 45 degrees and the length not more than 1 mm.

3.6.22 Smooth tip edge of reed if needed

If the tip edge seems to be too thick, you can reduce it to 0.30 mm by using the

---

between the wrapping ball and wire II. The author finishes the tube wrapping with a half-hitch, which is buried tightly under wire II. The string is then cut flush to wire II.

fine side of the sapphire file, moving gently with the grain of the reed. Make sure that the angle of the file is almost parallel to the blade, as in of Figure 3.14.

3.6.23 *Put wire I on loosely between wire II and collar;*
slide it and secure 30 mm from the tip edge

The bahn length (distance from wire I to the edge of the tip) for this reed is 30 mm. Measurement should be made from the side of wire I closest to the tip edge. Tighten wire I, but do not bend the twist down. Ensure that the twist of wire I is on the same side of the tube as the twist of wire III.

3.6.24 *Tune the reed*

The reed should blow A-440. If the pitch is higher, the aperture is too closed; therefore, open the tube by inserting pin mandrel #9. If the pitch is lower, tighten wire I.

3.6.25 *Apply two coats of glue*

Allow 20 minutes between coats; colored dope or nail polish can also be added.

3.6.26 *Let reed dry*

The drying process should take 48 hours naturally, or 12 hours if the reed is placed in an electric oven at the *warming* temperature of 65°C (150°F), or in a gas oven with a pilot light.

3.7 FINAL STAGE

3.7.1 *Tighten wire II*

Tighten wire II by pulling and twisting counterclockwise; clip wire III to binding and wire II to three turns. This re-tightening of wire II should be done while the reed is on the 10/12 mandrel, but 2 mm up from the mark. You will hear a cracking sound as the seal created by the cement around wire II is broken; the seal will be re-established in Section 3.8. File off the sharp edges of the wires.

3.7.2 *Tighten wire I*

Grasp wire I with pliers and allow the reed to settle into the mark made during forming. Make sure that the bahn length is still 30 mm. Tighten wire I by pulling and locking with two full twists. If wire I is still loose, tighten with one more half-twist. Fold wire I over toward butt, and file off sharp edges.

NOTE: A *full-twist* is a quarter turn, and a *half-twist* is an eighth of a turn. Wire I should not move when the reed is dry. However, when voicing and tuning the reed (Section 7.2), if wire I is too tight, it may cause the reed to be restricted in its vibrations. If that is the case, wire I should be replaced at that time.

3.7.3 Re-ream the tube

Use the drill reamer first, then the file reamer, as described in Step 3.6.17. The tube has dried and shrunk since the first reaming and therefore must be reamed again. Use a rattail file to remove loose fibers from inside the tube.

3.7.4 Correct side-slipping

If the tip edge has side-slipped, hold the reed at wire II and twist at wire III in the opposite direction of the side-slip.

3.7.5 Straighten sides, renew corners, and polish tip edge

The tip edge is polished by holding the reed vertically (with the tip down) on the table over a piece of 400 WD sandpaper. Squeeze the aperture closed and gently polish the tip edge. The sapphire file can be substituted for the 400 WD sandpaper.

3.8 FINAL TRIM

3.8.1 Tip undercut

Figure 3.15 shows the tip undercut procedure.

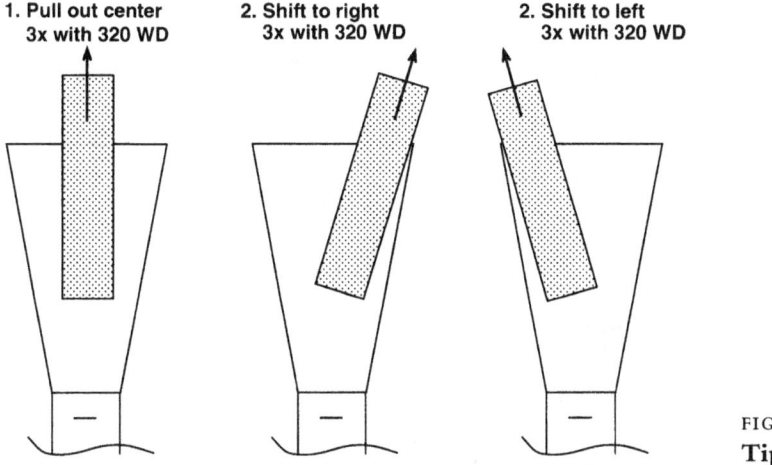

FIGURE 3.15
Tip undercut

a) Use a piece of 320 WD[19] sandpaper cut to 0.90 cm x 5.0 cm.

b) Examine tip edge; you will want to reduce its thickness by half.

c) Put 320 WD strip straight into reed as far as it will go. Press down on the

---

19. In the summer of 1990, Skinner said he used strips of 220 WD rather than 320 WD. Both will work: the 220 WD simply removes cane faster than 320 WD.

320 WD and tip with thumb *onto* forefinger. (Put forefinger onto work bench for support.)

d) Pull 320 WD out of the center of the reed, sloping slightly toward the outer surface. Then pull sandpaper strip similarly out of each side of the blade. Do not allow the sandpaper strip to go outside of the sides of the blades. Repeat procedure two or three times until the desired thickness of the tip edge has been achieved.

e) Repeat on other blade.

f) Under a lamp, check that a thin white strip across the tip can be seen.

3.8.2 Blades

Measure the blade thicknesses at the collar (30 mm, or 2 mm in front of collar if the Windsor Mill Process has been used), and at 43 mm and 50 mm. The thickness *after* the final trim should be:

30 mm	0.90 mm
43 mm	0.68 to 0.65 mm
50 mm	0.55 to 0.53 mm

Step 1: As needed, with the metal plaque inserted into the tip and using 220 WD sandpaper, gently blend the tip area into the 43-mm mark in the center of the blades. Allow the 220 WD to go over the tip edge of the cane onto the plaque. Start with five double strokes on both blades, then measure the thicknesses at 43 and 50 mm. The number of double strokes needed will depend on how much cane needs to be removed. If the thicknesses at 43 and 50 mm are thin enough, then do not take the sanding process back as far as the 43-mm mark. Simply blend the tip area into the 50-mm mark. As seen in Figure 3.16, a "V" is created in Step 1 and is eliminated in Step 2.

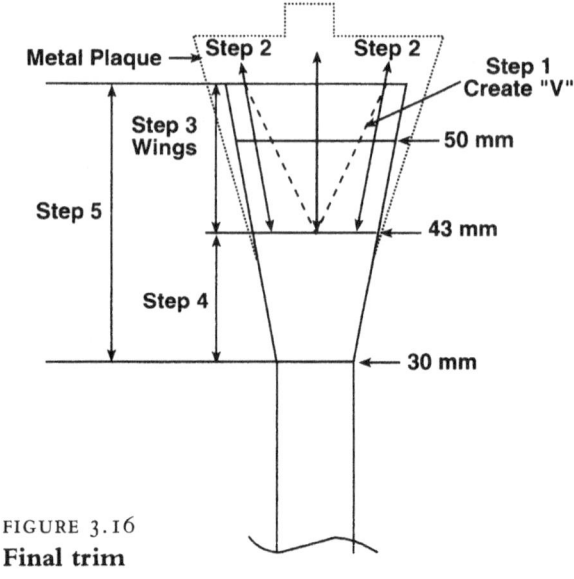

FIGURE 3.16 **Final trim**

Step 2: Repeat Step 1 on the sides of the blades, using the same number of strokes as in Step 1.

Step 3: *Without the metal plaque,* sand the wings with 220 WD, using five double strokes. Make sure that the fibers are not pyramided at the 43-mm mark.

Step 4: With 220 WD and no plaque, sand from 43 mm to the collar, using five double strokes.

Step 5: With 400 WD, sand both blades. *Leave the dust on the blades,* and polish the blades with the paper back of the sandpaper.

Step 6: Check the reed under a lamp and with a micrometer to make sure that the sides and wings are balanced, and that the measurements are correct. (Figure 3.1.)

3.8.3 *Using fast-drying household cement or colored dope, paint binding of reed, ensuring that seal is re-established at wire II*

3.8.4 *When glue is dry, soak reed for three or four minutes in water at room temperature*

Skinner recommended allowing the reed to soak fully with *capillary action.* The reed blades are submerged in warm water up to the collar. By capillary action, the reed will soak water into the tube as well. To promote capillary action, dip the butt end of the reed into the water before submerging the blades.

NOTE: The process of finishing the reed continues in Chapter 7, *Variations to the Outside of the Blades.*

CHAPTER 4

THE TIP TAPER REED: LOU SKINNER'S INTERPRETATION OF KNOCHENHAUER'S REED

4.1 PREPARATION OF TUBES, GOUGING, AND PROFILING

4.1.1 *Split cane longitudinally into four parts*

The tube of cane should be about 150 mm long, straight, and 24 to 26 mm in outside diameter. Split the cane lengthwise by pressing downward onto the end of the tube with a heavy knife while the tube is vertical to the bench. Split the cane first in half and then into quarters. If the cane is less than 24 mm in outside diameter, split it into three parts only.

4.1.2 *Soak cane for 12 hours at 20°C (68°F) or boil (for about one hour) until cane sinks*[20]

Besides softening the cane, soaking and/or boiling leaches out some of the sap and impurities.

4.1.3 *Cut cane to length for gouging machine*

Cut the cane to 120 mm, or 1 mm shorter than the gouger bed.

4.1.4 *Cut off sharp edges (fillier)*

Holding one end of the piece of cane, cut edges off each side, producing flats on each edge of the inside of the tube. Reverse the cane and repeat on the other end, so that the flats are consistent across the entire length of the cane. The cane should then fit in the gouger with the flats aligned with the top surface of the gouger bed.

---

20. At this point in Chapter 3, the Sink Method was inserted. Both methods are valid for both reeds, the choice being up to the individual.

4.1.5 *Gouge cane*

Gouge the cane while it is wet. The gouge should be eccentric, approximately 1.25 mm (±0.10 mm) in thickness in the center and 0.80 mm at the sides. If the cane is hard, use a thicker gouge (1.35 to 1.40 mm) and follow up with a deeper profile, since the softer part of the cane will be farther from the bark. Gouge the cane in both directions to compensate for lack of symmetry in the tubes.

NOTE: When ordering pre-gouged cane, request pieces 120 mm in length with an eccentric gouge 1.25 mm to 1.30 mm in the middle and a minimum of 0.80 mm at the edges.

4.1.5.a *Dry cane on 1-1/4-inch doweling for two to three days*

Attach four or five pieces of cane with elastic bands to 6-inch pieces of 1-1/4-inch hardwood doweling; dry for two or three days. Wet cane is dark, but dry cane is yellow.

4.1.6 *Profile cane by machine or by hand*

There are two methods of removing the bark between the collar marks: *profiling by machine* and *profiling by hand*. The machine method is outlined first.

4.1.6.a *Profiling by machine*

a) The cane should be profiled by machine while it is still wet. If the cane is dry, soak it for 2 hours in warm water before profiling. For a Tip Taper reed, the profiler should be set to produce the thicknesses as described in Figure 4.1.

NOTE: These measurements are for *dry* cane. Wet cane is approximately 0.03 mm thicker. Since the gouge is eccentric, it is not necessary to profile from side to side.

b) Smooth entire blade with 220 WD and finish with 400 WD.

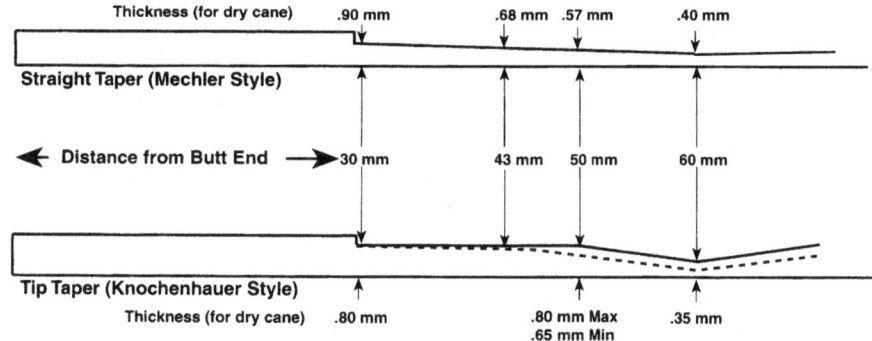

FIGURE 4.1 **Side view of Straight and Tip Taper profiles**

c) Add centerfold mark on the convex surface of the cane at 60 mm and gently score across the cane with a knife-edge file.

NOTE: When ordering profiled cane, vital *final measurements on dry cane* are a minimum of 0.80 mm in thickness at the collar and at 50 mm. The profile slopes from 0.80 mm thick at 50 mm to 0.35 mm thick in the center. It is also permissible to have a gentle slope from the collar at 0.80 mm to 50 mm **if the thickness at 50 mm is at least 0.65 mm**. The thickness at 50 mm would then slope to 0.35 mm in the center. Skinner stated that you should start the Tip Taper at the 50-mm mark of the blades in the profile even though ultimately the "shoulder" at 50 mm will be moved back to around 43 to 45 mm in the finished reed. In the summer of 1990, Skinner told the author that he profiled his Tip Taper reeds first as Straight Taper reeds. Then, with a second profiler, he added the tip taper, starting at the 50-mm mark. In order to obtain a Straight Taper profile with a thickness of 0.65 mm at 50 mm (two-thirds down the blade), the center would have to be at least 0.585 mm thick. The thicknesses should be about 0.05 mm thicker on the profile at this stage.

4.1.6.b *Profiling by hand*

Profiling by hand is not an uncommon practice and, for some bassoonists, provides more control over varying blade thicknesses.

a) Dry cane partially by placing it under a lamp for at least 20 minutes.

b) With dividers, mark the collar in the bark on the convex surface at 30 mm from each butt end.

c) Score the collar marks from one side of the cane to the other with a knife-edge file.

d) Place the cane on a wooden or Plexiglas easel (1 inch in diameter). Heavy elastic bands can be used to secure the butt ends. Choose a sharp, heavy knife; the heavier and wider the spine of the knife blade, the less likely the knife will *chatter* on the cane.

e) With the knife perpendicular to the cane, draw it back and forth between the collar marks in the center. The more secure the easel, the easier the profiling will be. (AUTHOR'S NOTE: *I place one end of the easel into a slot on the side of my bench, and secure it by wedging it in with my body weight and left hand holding underneath.*) Take the center of the cane down to 0.85 mm thickness. Each double stroke will remove approximately 0.10 mm of cane, so count your stokes and measure frequently.

f) Remove the bark on either side of the center strip and blend the side strips into the center so that the cane, when held to the light, appears to be evenly thick with no dark or heavy strips and areas. Smooth the entire profile with 220 WD.

g) With a pencil compass, mark 50 mm from each butt end. As seen from Figure 4.1, the thickness of the blade must be reduced to 0.80 mm at the 50-mm mark and to 0.35 at the centerfold (60 mm). This is done in two stages:

* With the knife, profile the center area between the 50-mm marks down to 0.50 mm, making sure that the strokes lighten at the 50-mm marks and get heavier in the center. Measure the thickness frequently. Six to eight double strokes should be sufficient. When the center is satisfactory, blend in the sides as above.

* Mark 55 mm from butt ends. Using 220 WD, take the mid-line down to 0.35 mm and blend in the sides.

h Smooth center portion of profile with 220 WD and smooth entire blade with 400 WD.

i) Add centerfold mark on cane at 60 mm and gently score across cane with knife-edge file.

4.1.7 *Tie profiled cane to a piece of doweling*

If the cane is still wet, tie to a piece of doweling 3.175 cm (1-1/4 inch) in diameter and let dry. The cane takes 12 hours to dry at room temperature, 6 hours in a warming oven or a gas oven with a pilot light, or 20 minutes directly under a 60-watt lamp. Using wet cane for the next steps is inadvisable, since drying causes shrinkage, making the measurements inaccurate.

4.2 PRE-TRIM

The inside of the gouge of the cane is critical both in the tube and blade areas. Alteration to the gouge—and consequently variations to the reed style—can take place at this point. The reed described here, however, has no alteration to the gouge if the Windsor Mill Process (Section 4.3) is left out.

4.2.1 *Smooth and polish inside of gouge with 400 WD sandpaper; leave the dust, and polish with the smooth paper side of the sandpaper*

4.2.2 *Shape cane*

See Step 3.2.2 for details.

4.2.3 *Mark collar and wire positions*

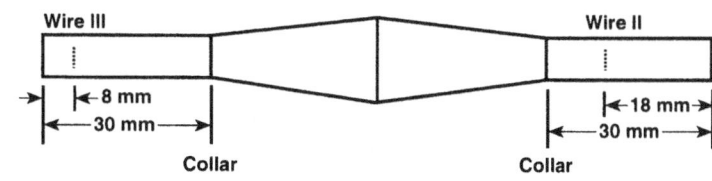

FIGURE 4.2
Collar and wire marks

With a pair of machine dividers, mark the points as described above (and shown in Figure 4.2), always measuring from the butt end. If necessary, enlarge the marks with a knife-edge file.

NOTE: Another common way that Skinner presented this reed was as the Del Negro model with wire I at 29 mm, or the bahn length at 27 mm; see the Del Negro model in Section 8.1.

4.3 ENHANCEMENT OF THE INSIDE OF THE TUBE (WINDSOR MILL PROCESS)[21]

The Windsor Mill Process, originally used by Skinner, involves removing cane from the inside of the tube, thus reducing the amount of pressure on the inside of the tube when it is forced around the mandrel. This method was designed to decrease the tendency of the outer surface of the tube to split. However, by disconnecting the fibers on the inside surface of the blades, the blades were allowed to vibrate more freely, especially at the lower frequencies. Although this process is, strictly speaking, a *variation* (Step 5.1.1) and, consequently, not required to make the reed, it is included here in a modified form because Skinner taught it with almost every reed style in the 1970s and 1980s. The *modification* is that the enhancement procedure here removes half as much cane, or 0.10 mm, as the *original* procedure, which cuts away 0.20 mm of cane.

4.3.1 *With pencil compass, mark the inside of gouge 32 mm from butt end*

4.3.2 *Pilot cut*

Measure the thickness of each butt and decrease by 0.10 mm. (If the butt is less than 1.20 mm thick, decrease it only to 1.10 mm.) Place the cane on a scraping board (a piece of cardboard tacked to a piece of wood) and scrape a pilot cut down the center from the 32-mm mark to the butt with the smallest scraper you have (#24, #20, or #16). Each stroke will remove approximately 0.01 mm, so count strokes and measure frequently (Figure 3.5).

4.3.3 *Superimposed cut*

With a pencil, draw a sawtooth line from 32 mm to the butt (Figure 3.6). Superimpose scraper #32 onto the original pilot cut, scraping from the 32-mm mark to off the butt end, until pencil marks are removed (Figure 3.5).

4.3.4 *Sand entire inside butt with 200 DRY and 400 WD*

---

21. This portion of the process is presented as Skinner approved it in 1988, and as it appeared in the handout for the lecture at the 1994 IDRS meeting. Note that if you chose to do the Sink Method, you do not need to do the Windsor Mill.

Smooth out the transition from the Windsor Mill enhancement slightly into the blades.

4.3.5 *Define collar of reed*

When you use machine-profiled cane, you will need to remove the burr between the collar and the blade. Place the cane on the easel and score the collar mark (30 mm from the butt) across the tube with a knife-edge file. *Do not chip out the burr yet!*

4.4 CENTER-PANEL SCORING

Figure 4.3 shows the score marks for the center-panel scoring.

a) With machine dividers, put a short mark approximately 0.50 mm long on the bark of the tube, parallel to the sides, inset 3 mm from each side, and running from the collar mark toward the butt, as in Figure 4.3.

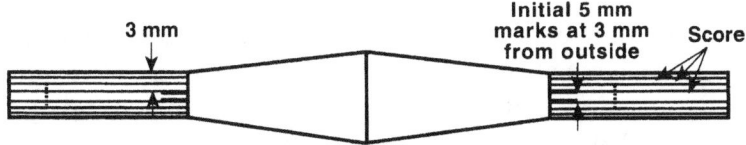

FIGURE 4.3 **Center-panel scoring**

b) Score the cane along each 3-mm mark to the butt end. To do this, use the tip of an Exacto knife to penetrate the bark lightly in a line running down and past the butt at right angles to the collar. This is most easily accomplished if you place the cane on the easel and the easel on the table.

c) Score two more lines, parallel to the first, between the edge of the cane and each 3-mm score line.

d) In the final 1 mm at the butt end of each score line, press the Exacto blade right through the cane. It is essential that the score lines all have the same depth and run parallel. The scoring need be only deep enough to penetrate the bark (about 0.20 mm). If all the score marks are not parallel and even in depth, the tube will form unevenly when the mandrel is inserted (Step 4.6.5), causing pressure ridges and ruining the balance in the blades. The tube could even split into the blades, causing an irreparable air leak.

e) Chip out the burr of bark in front of the collar; use an Exacto knife, with the cane on the easel. Be careful to continue the thickness of the profile of the blades into the collar. Do not allow the cane to become gradually thicker or thinner at this point by sloping up or down to the collar. Smooth out the area in front of the collar with a sapphire file.

4.5 PARALLEL-SIDES PRE-TRIM

This portion of the method is the final and most critical stage of profiling. The blades of the reed are prepared so that they will vibrate freely as a blank as soon as the tip is cut.

NOTE: The following measurements are *minimum thicknesses* of the spine of the blades when the parallel-sides pre-trim is finished (measurements on dry cane):

at collar	0.90 to 0.80 mm (measure collar thicknesses 2 mm in front of collar if the Windsor Mill enhancement has been used)
at 43 mm	0.70 to 0.80 mm
at 50 mm	0.65 to 0.80 mm
at 60 mm (center)	0.35 to 0.40 mm

4.5.1 *Mark blades and decrease thickness of profile*

    a) With a pencil compass, mark 43 mm and 50 mm (from butt ends) on the top and underside of each blade.

    b) Using a heavy knife with the blade at right angles to the surface of the cane, reduce the thickness of the center portion of the profile (from the collar to the 43-mm mark) so that the blades measure 0.80 mm at 2 mm in front of the collar, and 0.80 mm at the 43-mm mark.

OR

    Slope the thickness of the center portion of the profile (from the collar to the 50-mm mark) so that the blades measure 0.80 mm at 2 mm in front of the collar, and 0.65 mm at the 50-mm mark. If using this latter procedure here, lighter strokes should be used later in Step 4.5.4, Pre-trim.

    c) If the cane appears to be exceptionally brittle, make the whole blade thinner by another 0.03 mm.

4.5.2 *Decrease thickness of sides of blade by one-half to no thinner than 0.40 mm at the edge*

    a) Set pencil compass to 3 mm and mark along blades from collar to reed tip, as shown in Figure 4.4.

    b) Determine the thickness of the side of the blades.

    c) With the cane on the easel, hold the

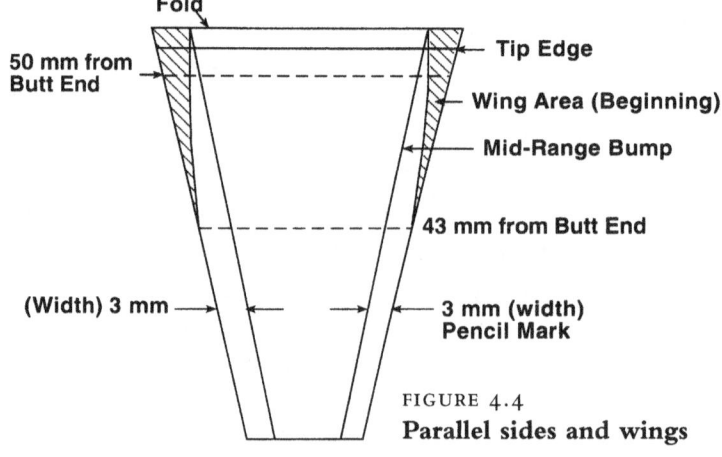

FIGURE 4.4
Parallel sides and wings

heavy knife vertically to the cane and pull from the collar to the 50-mm mark parallel to the sides of the shape. Make strokes in one direction only, from the collar to the 50-mm mark, and count the number of strokes (approximately 10) so that you can use the same number of strokes on the other three quadrants. Use more strokes on each quadrant if needed. The sides of the blades should be approximately 0.40 mm thick and should slope upward to the 3-mm mark parallel to the shape.

4.5.3 *Remove mid-range bump*

Because of Step 4.5.2, you can now see a ridge along roughly the 3-mm mark which parallels the shape. The ridge is removed by gently pulling the knife from the collar to the 50-mm mark, this time parallel with the fibers and not parallel to the sides of the shape. This procedure also begins to establish the wing area. Again, pull only from the collar to the 50-mm mark.

NOTE: The tip edge and wing area do not require much thinning at all.

4.5.4 *Pre-trim*

Proceed as follows and as shown in Figure 4.5, *Pre-trim beginning*.

a) With the cane on the easel, pull the heavy knife from the collar to the fold and back, starting the first stroke at line 1, as indicated in Figure 4.5 (approximately 3 mm in from the edge), and proceeding toward the side, stroke to line 8.

b) Retrace the eight strokes and proceed with three more to the center line (-1, -2, -3).

c) Repeat for each quadrant.

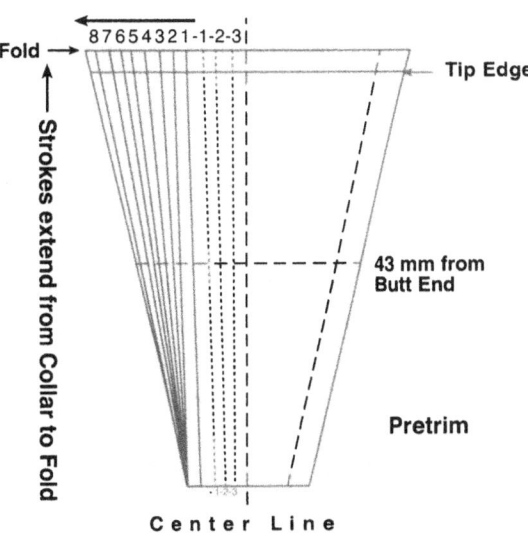

FIGURE 4.5 **Pre-trim beginning**

4.5.5 *Sand entire surface lightly with 120 DRY*

This sanding will smooth out surfaces that were made uneven by the knife work, and will establish a gentle curvature from the center line to the sides.

4.5.6 *Establish wings*

On each blade, mark 43 mm (from the butt end) with a pencil compass, as in Figure 4.6. Using 120 WD, sand the wing areas, creating a knife edge on the sides from the collar to the fold. However, be careful not to make the edges so thin that the sides disappear. In addition, checking the cane in the light, you should begin to establish the tongue by blending the wings into the center of the tip area.

NOTE: The tendency is to take out too much cane at this stage!

4.5.7 *Eliminate pyramided fibers*

Using the heavy knife, smooth down the pyramided fibers just in front of the 43-mm mark (Figure 4.6). Pyramided fibers, or a sudden thickening of the cane at this point, will prevent the low pitches from responding.

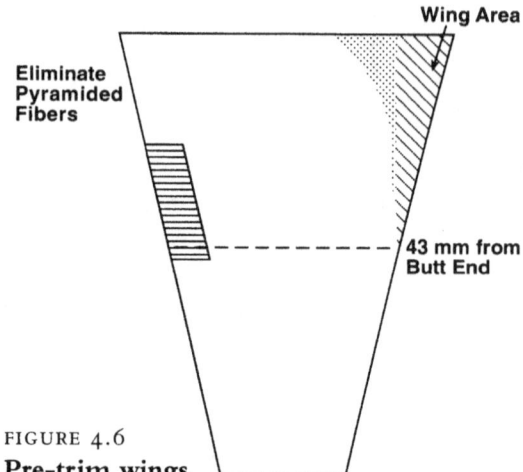

FIGURE 4.6
Pre-trim wings

4.5.8 *Sand pyramided fibers*

Use 120 DRY to remove bumps from knife work and sand overall with 220 WD.

4.5.9 *Re-establish fold line with knife-edge file*

4.5.10 *Soak cane for 10 to 12 hours or until it sinks*

4.6 FORMING AND DRYING [22]

4.6.1 *Fold and remove flare*

Grasp the reed (with thumbs underneath and forefingers on top, equidistant on each side of the centerfold); fold reed with concave sides inward. If necessary, roll the fold so that the collars are lined up. While holding the two halves of the reed together, remove the flare from the tube with the Exacto knife so that the sides of the tube are parallel. (On the Fox and Knochenhauer shapes, the tube flares outward from the narrowest point at the wire II mark to the butt. This step removes that flare.)

NOTE: Beveling can be added here, even with the flare removed (Section 5.5 *Beveling Variation*). However, Skinner did not include beveling at this point when working on the book.

---

22. For a method of forming and drying that does not remove the flare, see Section 8.7. Also, for a discussion on beveling (which is not required on reeds where the flare has been removed), see Section 5.5. This book implies that a single reed is made from the beginning to end by itself. Skinner, of course, had cane and reeds at several stages simultaneously. To keep the cane and string soaked, and to heat the mandrel (4.6.1 to 4.6.15), and to soak the reed (4.8.4), he used a hot pot with a thermostat set to keep the water at approximately 90°C/194°F.

4.6.2 Side-slip top blade to left at butt about 1 to 2 mm; pinch tip edge of reed

While holding the reed so that the butt is pointing toward your body, and the tip edge is pointing away, side-slip the butt of the top blade to the left about 1 to 2 mm. This procedure allows the halves of the tube and the blades to fit together better because one side of the tube will be slightly buried inside the other. The effect of the 1 to 2 mm side-slip will be lessened when the forming mandrel is inserted and turned clockwise.

4.6.3 Wrap reed, starting at collar and proceeding to 3 mm from butt end; finish with slipknot

This wrapping is essential so that the tube of the reed will be formed evenly. Use the same cotton crochet thread that you will finally use to finish wrapping the reed. Begin by laying the standing end of the thread on the upper side of the tube at the collar and wrap two courses or revolutions over it. This should secure the thread. Continue wrapping carefully and tightly toward the butt end, making sure each course is laid evenly beside the previous course. Do not allow any course to override a neighboring course. Finish with a slipknot.

4.6.4 Place reed in hot water (90°C/194°F) for 20 minutes

Heat the 10/12 mandrel in the water for the last 30 seconds.

4.6.5 Insert the forming mandrel

Place the 10/12 mandrel into the aperture of the butt end slowly but firmly, up to the mark, gently twisting the mandrel clockwise as needed. Begin by grasping the reed on the sides of the wire III mark with thumb and forefinger. Start pushing the mandrel in gently at first. Make sure that the mandrel goes in straight and not at an angle. Pushing the mandrel in at an angle could cause one side of the tube to arch and crack more than the other. A certain amount of cracking is almost inevitable in the tube (Section 4.4 on *Central Panel Scoring*). The cracking may extend into the blade, but as long as the crack remains on the surface of the cane and does not go right through, the reed is salvageable. Any pressure ridges that are created because of a crack in the surface of the tube must be taken care of in the final trim by removing cane from the blade (with a sapphire file) at the point in the collar where the split enters the blade.

4.6.6 Partially unwrap string from butt end to just beyond wire III mark; put on wire III

Pull the string counterclockwise to maintain the tension of the slipknot. Wrap the wire counterclockwise two full turns,[23] making sure that the courses are adjacent and not overlapping.

---

23. Skinner considered a "full turn" to be one complete revolution of the wires accomplished with the fingers. A "full twist" is a 1/4 turn, using pliers. A "half twist" is therefore 1/8 of a turn, using pliers.

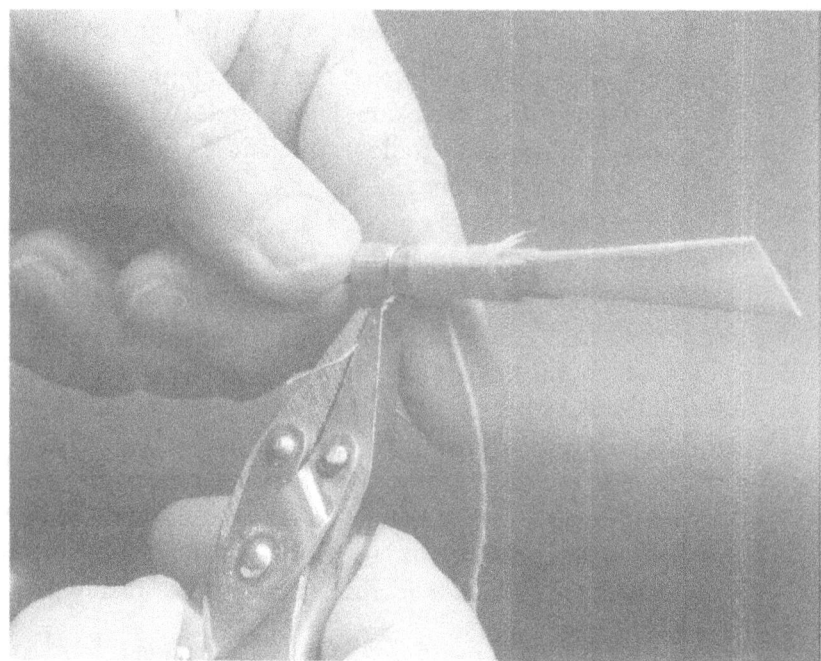

FIGURE 4.7 **Partially unwrapping string and putting on wire III**

With your fingers, twist both ends of the wire counterclockwise one or two full turns (Figure 4.7). Tighten with pliers by pulling the twisted wire away from the tube and twisting counterclockwise to snug; four or five full twists should be sufficient. Always pull to tighten and twist to snug. Clip off excess wire above four or five turns.

4.6.7 *Remove string and soak string in water*

Soak the cotton string first: when the string has been put back on the reed and dries, it will shrink tightly around the tube, helping to make a well-formed airtight tube.

4.6.8 *With machine dividers, mark full fundamental length, the distance from wire II mark to tip edge, on the blade at 38 mm*

4.6.9 *Put on wire II*

Follow the same procedures as given in Step 4.6.6, but make sure that the twist of wire II is on the opposite side of the tube from wire III. Pull to tighten, twist (counterclockwise) to lock. Make sure that the tip-edge side of wire II is at the mark. Since the vibrations begin at the tip edge of the reed, wires will affect vibrations beginning on the side of the wire closest to the tip. Therefore, measurements for the bahn length refer to the distance from the tip edge of the cane to the side of wire I nearest the tip.

4.6.10 Butt molding

With parallel-jaw pliers, gently mold the butt all the way around the mandrel from wire III to off the end.

4.6.11 Center-panel molding

Gently mold the center of the tube, not the sides, between wires II and III around the mandrel with parallel jaw pliers.

4.6.12 Retighten wires II and III and remove overlap on outside edge of cane between wire II and collar

The overlap on the edge of the cane is removed (with an Exacto knife) to make sure that wire I, when it is put on, will conform as closely as possible to the tube, as in Figure 4.8.

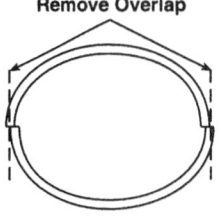

FIGURE 4.8
Cross-section of tube at wire I, showing removal of overlap

4.6.13 Narrow the tip edge to 15 mm if needed

This step can be accomplished by filing gently with a sapphire file from the collar to the tip on the sides of the shape. Use the coarse or fine side of the sapphire file, depending on how much cane has to be removed. The tip edge (marked as Full Fundamental Length) should be no less than 15 mm wide. If a flatter pitch is desired, the tip edge should be left at 15.5 mm at this stage; the reed can be narrowed later.

4.6.14 With knife-edge file, cut in adjustment notches (four or five) between wires II and III on center and sides of tube

Adjustment notches (Figure 4.9) are essential for later alterations to the tube between wires II and III, which will affect response and pitch.

4.6.15 While reed and string are wet, put binding on reed[24]

---

24. Most bassoonists put a wrapping of string over wire III, sometimes referred to as a "turk's head." There are almost as many variations of this wrapping as there are reed makers. The purpose of the wrapping is to allow the player to grasp the reed and, to a lesser extent, to keep the reed intact. Placing the reed on a holding mandrel, the author begins by looping the cotton string onto the upturned twist of wire III. The string is then pulled tightly and laid beside the blade side of wire III for 1-1/4 revolutions. The string is then crossed diagonally over wire III to the butt side. A string is laid down for a half-revolution beside wire III and is then brought diagonally back to the blade side for another half-revolution. When the first diagonal cross-over is reached, the string is laid just

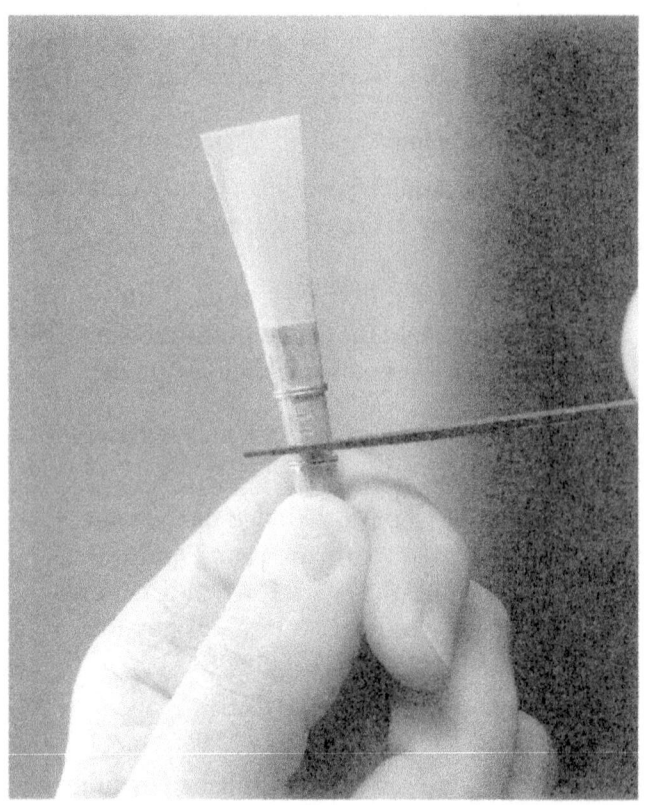

FIGURE 4.9
Adjustment notches

4.6.16 File butt end of reed flat so reed can stand vertically

4.6.17 Ream reed with drill and file reamers

Push the drill reamer in, twisting clockwise to 18 mm (wire II). The file reamer is inserted 17 mm, twisting counterclockwise. Use of these tools can be facilitated by putting tape on the shafts to mark the depth measurements.

4.6.18 Straighten sides

If the sides of the shape have twisted apart as a result of reaming, realign them by twisting wire III with the forming mandrel in, or by straightening the sides again with a sapphire file.

---

beyond and beside (not on top of) this cross-over, and returned to the butt side of wire III. The author continues this process until wire III is no longer visible. At this point, 2 complete revolutions of string are made around the tube on the butt side of the wrapping. A third revolution overlaps the 2 and returns the string to the ball for the last diagonal cross-over. The last diagonal cross-over on the blade side begins a single layer of tightly wrapped string around the reed tube, filling in the space between the wrapping ball and wire II. The author finishes the tube wrapping with a half-hitch, which is buried tightly under wire II. The string is then cut flush to wire II.

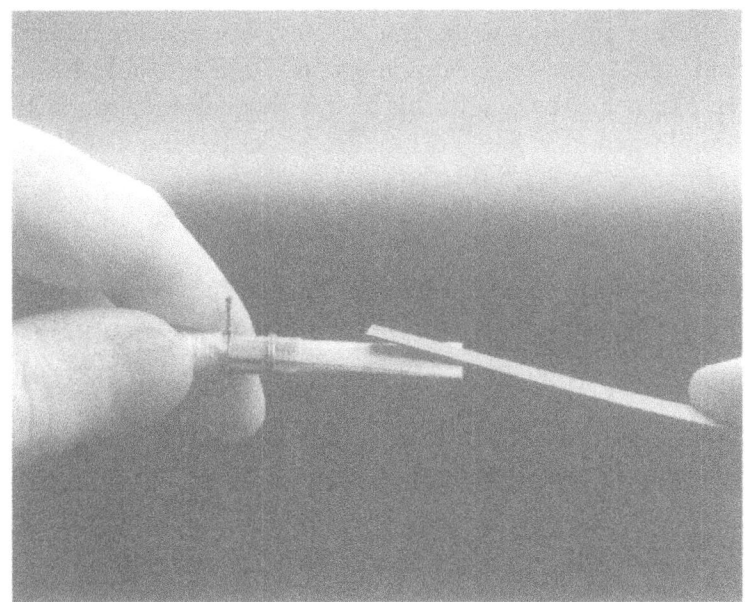

FIGURE 4.10
Sapphire file on tip edge

4.6.19 Cut reed

This can be done with a knife and cutting block, with a pair of 5-inch jeweller's end-nippers, or with a tip cutter. Cut the reed at *Full Fundamental Length:* 38 mm from wire II or 56 mm from the butt.

4.6.20 Adjust side-slipping

To ensure that the reed does not leak, adjust the side-slipping of the blades so that the upper right side is slightly inside the lower right when viewed from the butt end. The tip is not side-slipped.

4.6.21 Clip corners of reed

The angle should be 45 degrees and the length not more than 1 mm.

4.6.22 Smooth tip edge of reed if needed

If the tip edge of the reed seems too thick, you can reduce it to 0.30 by using the fine side of the sapphire file, moving gently with the grain of the reed. Make sure that the angle of the file is almost parallel to the blade, as in Figure 4.10.

4.6.23 Put on wire I loosely between wire II and collar; slide it and secure 30 mm from tip edge

The bahn length (distance from wire I to the tip edge) for this reed is 30 mm. Measurement should be made from the side of wire I closest to the tip edge. Tighten wire I, but do not bend the twist down. Ensure that the twist of wire I is on the same side of the tube as the twist of wire III.

NOTE: The reed described in this chapter is a "C reed" because the natural (low) pitch of the reed is C, based on a bahn length of 30 mm (Table 1.1 in Chapter 1). However, Skinner often taught this reed with a bahn length of 27 mm, producing a natural pitch of E flat. This model was called the *Del Negro model* and is described in Section 8.1.

4.6.24 *Tune the reed*

The reed should blow A-440. If the pitch is higher, the aperture is too closed; therefore, open the tube by inserting pin mandrel #9. If the pitch is lower, tighten wire I.

4.6.25 *Apply two coats of glue*

Allow 20 minutes between coats; colored dope or nail polish can also be added.

4.6.26 *Let reed dry*

The drying process should take 48 hours naturally, or 12 hours if the reed is placed in an electric oven at the warming temperature of 65°C (150°F), or in a gas oven with a pilot light.

4.7 FINAL STAGE

4.7.1 *Tighten wire II*

Tighten wire II by pulling and twisting counterclockwise; clip wire III to binding and wire II to three turns. This re-tightening of wire II should be done while the reed is on the 10/12 mandrel, but 2 mm up from the mark. You will hear a cracking sound as the seal created by the cement around wire II is broken. The seal will be re-established in Section 4.8. File off the sharp edges of the wires.

4.7.2 *Tighten wire I*

Grasp wire I with pliers and allow reed to settle into mark made during forming. Make sure that the bahn length is still 30 mm. Tighten wire I by pulling and locking with two full twists. If wire I is still loose, tighten with one more half-twist. Fold wire I over toward the butt, and file off the sharp edges.

NOTE: A *full-twist* is a quarter turn, and a *half-twist* is an eighth of a turn. Wire I should not move when the reed is dry. However, when voicing and tuning the reed (Section 7.2), if wire I is too tight, it may cause the reed to be restricted in its vibrations. If that is the case, wire I should be replaced at this time.

4.7.3 *Re-ream the tube*

Use the drill reamer first, then the file reamer, as described in Step 4.6.17. The tube has dried and shrunk since the first reaming and therefore must be reamed again. Use a rattail file to remove loose fibers from inside the tube.

4.7.4 Correct side-slipping

If the tip edge has side-slipped, hold the reed at wire II and twist at wire III in the opposite direction of the side-slip.

4.7.5 Straighten sides, renew corners, and polish tip edge

The tip edge is polished by holding the reed vertically (with the tip down) on the table over a piece of 400 WD sandpaper. Squeeze the aperture closed and gently polish the tip edge. The sapphire file can be substituted for the 400 WD sandpaper.

4.8 FINAL TRIM

4.8.1 OMIT tip undercut

4.8.2 Blades

Measure blade thicknesses at the collar (30 mm, or 2 mm in front of collar if the Windsor Mill Process has been used), and at 43 mm and 50 mm. The thickness *after* the final trim should be:

30 mm	0.90 to 0.80 mm
43 mm	0.68 to 0.65 mm
50 mm	0.55 to 0.53 mm

Step 1: As needed, with the metal plaque inserted into the tip and using 220 WD sandpaper, gently blend the tip area into the 43-mm mark in the center of the blades. Allow the 220 WD to go over the tip edge of the cane onto the plaque. Start with five double strokes on both blades, then measure the thicknesses at 43 and 50 mm. The number of double strokes needed will depend on how much cane needs to be removed. If the thicknesses at 43 and 50 mm are thin enough, then do not take the sanding process back as far as the 43-mm mark. Simply blend the tip area into the 50-mm mark. As seen in Figure 4.11, a "V" is created in Step 1 and is eliminated in Step 2.

Step 2: Repeat Step 1 on the sides of the blades, using the same number of strokes as in Step 1.

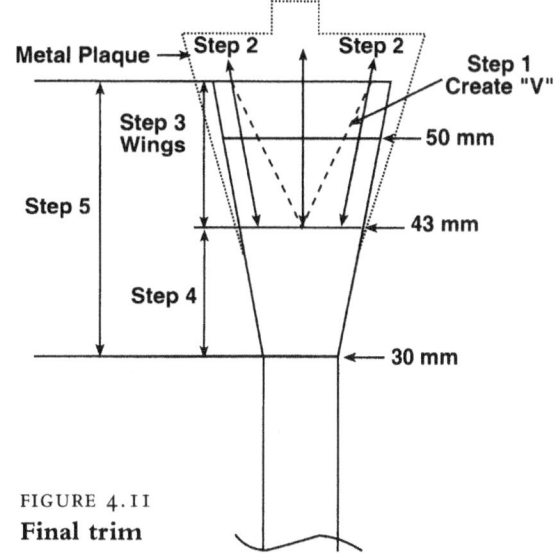

FIGURE 4.11
Final trim

Step 3: *Without the metal plaque,* sand the wings with 220 WD, using five double strokes. Make sure that the fibers are not pyramided at the 43-mm mark.

Step 4: With 220 WD and no plaque, sand from 43 mm to the collar, using five double strokes.

Step 5: With 400 WD, sand both blades. *Leave the dust on the blades,* and polish the blades with the paper back of the sandpaper.

Step 6: Check the reed under a lamp and with a micrometer to make sure that the sides and wings are balanced, and that the measurements are correct (*see* Figure 4.1).

4.8.3 *Using fast-drying household cement or colored dope, paint binding of reed, ensuring that seal is re-established at wire II*

4.8.4 *When glue is dry, soak reed for three or four minutes in water at room temperature*

Skinner recommended allowing the reed to soak fully with *capillary action.* The reed blades are submerged in warm water up to the collar. By capillary action, the reed will soak water into the tube as well. To promote capillary action, dip the butt end of the reed into the water before submerging the blades.

NOTE: The process of finishing the reed continues in Chapter 7, *Variations to the Outside of the Blades.*

CHAPTER 5[25]

VARIATIONS TO THE TUBE

For the purposes of this chapter, the tube is that part of the reed from the collar to the butt end. Skinner considered enhancements to this part of the reed primarily as ways of reducing cracking in the cane, and especially of keeping cracks from running into the blades. Of course, these variations also affect the way the blades vibrate and, consequently, how the reed sounds.

At various points in this chapter, specific steps are presented along with the numbers (e.g., 3.4.1 or 4.4.1) indicating where these steps should be added or substituted in Chapters 3 or 4.

5.1 THE WINDSOR MILL PROCESS: ORIGINAL VERSION[26]

This variation was developed and used by Skinner, and taught to most of his students, as an alternative to the Sink Method. However, it is interesting to note that Skinner was flexible in its application (Preface, page xviii). The Windsor Mill Process was originally used as a way to prevent cracks (primarily in the bark of the tube) from travelling into the blades. This was done by removing cane from the inside of the tube. Since fewer fibers are compressed on the inside of the tube when it is forced around the forming mandrel, there is less internal pressure on the bark, and therefore less splitting, and fewer cracks running into the blades.

---

25. In Chapters 5, 6, and 8, the variation or reed model is first discussed and then presented as a method. The numbers in italics refer to the relevant steps in Chapters 3 and 4. The first number refers to the chapter. The steps of the method are designed to replace those steps described in Chapters 3 and 4.

26. Skinner derived the term Windsor Mill Process from the fact that he and his wife lived on Windsor Mill Drive in Baltimore when he first conceived of the idea.

The *Windsor Mill Process*, however, also has the effect of undampening the reed linearly, thus making it easier to blow. Since the fibers on the inside surface of the blades are shortened at the collar (or, to be precise, 2 mm in front of the collar), these fibers vibrate more freely than the fibers on the outer surface of the blades, which are still connected to the tube. Furthermore, this linear undampening effect is directly related to the amount of cane removed from the tube: the more cane out, the greater the effect. In addition, removing the cane will allow slightly more space on the inside of the reed—from where the cane removal starts to where the bocal is inserted (up to 18 mm or wire II). This increase of internal space and the disconnection of inside fibers will drop the overall pitch of the crows of the reed. This effect will be even more noticeable if cane removal is extended farther into the blades than 2 mm.

Method

> *3.3.1 or 4.3.1   With pencil compass, mark the inside of the gouge 32 mm from butt end.*
>
> *3.3.2 or 4.3.2   Pilot cut*
>
> Measure the thickness of each butt and decrease by 0.20 mm. (If the butt is less than 1.20 mm thick, decrease it only to 1.10 mm.) Place the cane on a scraping board (a piece of cardboard tacked to a piece of wood) and scrape a pilot cut down the center from the 32-mm mark to the butt with the smallest scraper you have (#24, #20, or #16). Each stroke will remove approximately 0.01 mm, so count strokes and measure frequently.
>
> *3.3.3 or 4.3.3 Superimposed cut*
>
> With a pencil, draw a sawtooth line from 32 mm to the butt (Figure 3.6). Superimpose scraper #32 onto the original pilot cut, scraping from the 32-mm mark to off the butt end until the pencil marks are removed.
>
> *3.3.4 or 4.3.4 Sand entire inside butt with 400 WD.*
>
> Smooth out the transition from the Windsor Mill enhancement slightly into the blades.
>
> *3.3.5 or 4.3.5 Define collar of reed.*
>
> When you use machine-profiled cane, you will need to remove the burr between the collar and the blade. Place the cane on the easel and score the collar mark (30 mm from the butt) across the tube with a knife-edge file. *Do not chip out the burr yet!*

5.2 REVERSE CORONA VARIATION

This variation is designed to pull the sides of the tube more tightly together by thinning and therefore weakening the sides. Because the effects transfer into the blades, this variation enables the blades to *bury* the sides more tightly in front of the collar, allowing the tube to be rounder. Because the overall effect will be to dampen the reed, giving it a darker quality and a rounder tube, this variation compliments the Tip Taper reed more than the Straight Taper reed.

Method

4.3.1   With a pencil compass, mark the collar on the inside of the tube at 30 mm from the butt end.

4.3.2   With a scraper larger than the inside diameter of the cane (e.g., #40), scrape from the collar mark to the butt end ten times on both sides.

FIGURE 5.1 **Reverse Corona variation**

4.3.3   From 3 to 5 mm into the blade, scrape a transitional slope to the tube following the shape (Figure 5.1).

4.3.4   As in Figure 3.6, draw a sawtooth line down the center of the tube from the collar mark to the butt end. With a #32 scraper, scrape the tube from the collar mark to the butt end until the pencil mark disappears. This will re-establish an inside diameter in the tube of 2.54 mm. Smooth with 220 DRY and 400 WD.

5.3 FOUR FLATS WITH TAKE-OUT VARIATION

This process removes cane from the edge of the tube from the collar to the butt, thus opening up the space on the inside of the tube, and leaving the sides stronger at the collar as compared to the Reverse Corona variation. The overall effect of the Four Flats with Take-Out variation will be to free up the vibrations of the blades, creating a brighter timbre and a more easily blowing reed.

Method

3.3.1 or 4.3.1   With a pencil compass, put the collar mark at 30 mm on the inside of the tube, and another mark at 35 mm into the blades.

3.3.2 or 4.3.2   *With a sapphire file, flatten the edges of the tube and 5 mm into the blades (Figure 5.2). The flat sides of the tube should be between 1 and 1.5 mm wide and should taper to nothing, 5 mm into the blades.*

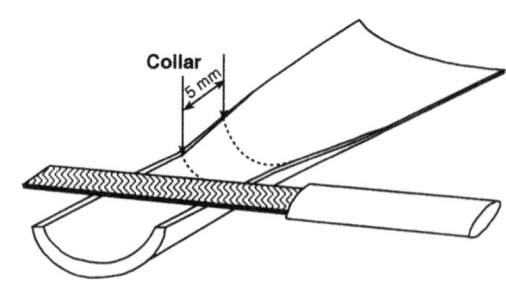

FIGURE 5.2 **Four Flats with Take-Out varia-**

3.3.3 or 4.3.3   *With a small scraper (#16 or #20), take out the "bump" or shoulder from the inside of the flattened edge (see Figure 5.3).*

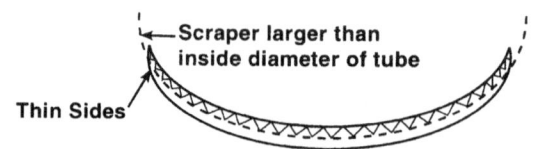

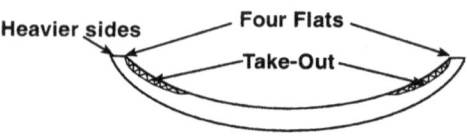

FIGURE 5.3 **Comparison of the Reverse Corona with Four Flats with Take-Out**

3.3.4 or 4.3.4   *Re-establish a 2.54-mm radius on the inside of the tube from collar to butt. Smooth with 200 DRY and 400 WD.*

5.4 TUBE TAPER

This variation is an alternative to the removal of the flare from the shape and sideslipping as described in Step 3.6.1 and Step 4.6.1 (*see also* Section 8.7). Leaving the flare on the shape has the effect of causing the aperture to close. This variation counters that tendency by thinning the tube and allowing wire III to be pulled in more tightly; thus, wire III uses wire II as a "fulcrum," causing the aperture to open. The gentle cone shape on the inside of the butt fits the Heckel bocal well, without having to do the extensive file reaming described in Step 3.6.17 and Step 4.6.17. This variation is accomplished by re-gouging the shaped and profiled cane as follows.

Method

3.3.1 or 4.3.1 Mark 18 mm (wire II) from the butt end on the inside of each side of the shaped cane.

3.3.2 or 4.3.2 At the far end of the gouger bed, place tape 9 mm wide by 20 mm long by approximately 0.30 mm or 0.32 mm thick (three layers of masking tape). This thickness will put the cane at an angle, creating a taper when it is re-gouged.

3.3.3 or 4.3.3 Re-gouge each side of the tube from the 18-mm mark to the butt; drop the thickness of the butt by 0.4 mm.

NOTE 1: This variation can also be accomplished by using a #24 (3/4 inch) scraper wheel.

NOTE 2: For Step 3.6.5 or Step 4.6.5, *Inserting the forming mandrel*, use the #13 mandrel for the Tube-Taper variation.

5.5 BEVELING VARIATION

Beveling is required on butts where the flare has *not* been removed but can be done on *any* reed. This variation can be understood as an alternative to the Tube Taper and to removing the flare. It consists of removing an increasingly larger amount of cane from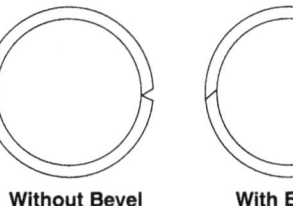

FIGURE 5.4
Butt end of the reed with and without beveling

the inside edge of the tube from 18 mm (wire II) to the butt (or from the collar to the butt) on opposite quadrants of the tube. Often used by Carl Mechler, this process allows the *sealing edges* of the tube to be at the same angle, as seen in Figure 5.4.

Method

3.4.1 or 4.4.1 With an Exacto knife, and starting 18 mm from the butt end, take out the right inside edge of the tube, increasing the amount of cane as you proceed to the butt

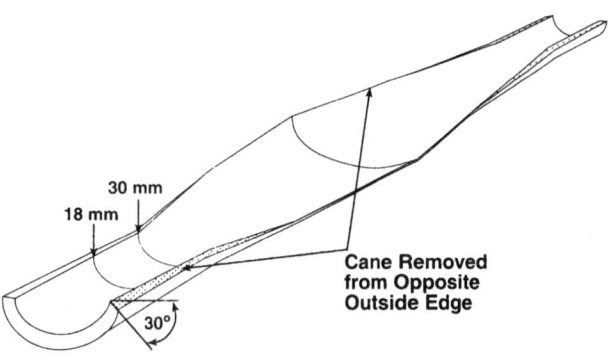

FIGURE 5.5 **Beveling**

end, as in Figure 5.5. The angle should be 30 degrees. If the top blade is side-slipped to the left by 1 or 2 mm, then when the forming mandrel is

> *inserted and twisted clockwise, the unbeveled edge will bury itself inside the beveled edge.*

Chip Kaufmann, a later student and friend of Skinner's, informed the author that Skinner talked about a *Right Chamfer* which consisted of taking cane out at a 45° angle on the right side of each tube half similar to beveling but with the cane coming out of the bark on the upper edge of the tube from the collar to the butt. Kaufmann said that Skinner told him that a *Right Chamfer* replaces a "Reverse Corona." Because a *Right Chamfer* does not change the radius inside the tube, resiliency as a result of forming the tube is reduced, and more space is left giving the reed a deeper sound. This variation is especially useful on the Straight Taper reed where the sides at the collar are left heavy. While Skinner did not include beveling in the chapters that he approved or in his later handout, the author's notes predating 1985 and the tapes from the summer of 1990 show that Skinner did discuss beveling as a variation to the tube described above. Basically, beveling is optional if you *remove* the flare from the shape; if you *keep* the flare on the shape, beveling or a Tube Taper is required.

CHAPTER 6[27]

VARIATIONS TO THE GOUGE AND TO THE INSIDE OF THE BLADES AND TUBES

Essentially, these variations enhance the gouge by trimming the reed on the inside of the blades, especially in the case of *linear enhancements*, the *Dip Tip*, and the *Vivaldi* variation of the *flutes*. These procedures are carried out on the *inside* of the cane before profiling and are organized into three categories: *linear enhancements*, with cane removed, relative to the bark, sloping from the collar (thick) to the tip edge (thin); *Dip Tip*, with cane sloping in the opposite way, from the tip edge (thick) to the collar (thin); and *flutes*, with cane removed parallel to the bark either between the collar marks or throughout the entire gouge. In addition, there are two variations—the *Sandboard* and *Even Down About Shape*—which alter the gouge by taking cane out from the inside of the blades parallel to the shape, in effect making the gouge in the front part of the blades more elliptical. For the variations in this chapter (with the exception of the Dip Tip), it is assumed that the beginning gouge is eccentric and at least 1.25 mm thick.

6.1 LINEAR ENHANCEMENTS (LE)

The cane on the inside of the tube is taken out in a slope or taper, starting from near the collar mark and becoming gradually thinner toward the tip of the blade. All linear enhancements are by definition dampening procedures because they create pyramided fibers on the inside surface of the blades (Section 1.3, *The Resiliency of Cane and Fibers*).[28] When the reed is profiled with linear enhancement, the cane toward the tip edge will be cut closer to the bark (and will consequently be harder) than the cane closer to the

---

27. In Chapters 5, 6, and 8, the variation or reed model is first discussed and then presented as a method. The numbers in italics refer to the relevant steps in Chapters 3 and 4. The first number refers to the chapter. The steps of the method are designed to replace those steps in Chapters 3 and 4.

28. Profiling is, of course, a sort of linear enhancement that is done to the outside of the blades. However, Skinner considered the Linear Enhancement (LE) variations to be Linear Dampening (LD), and to be a fundamentally internal procedure. He considered Lateral or Horizontal Damp-

collar. This means that the tip edge can be made very thin and that the reed will pop open easily. The simplest example of a linear enhancement, or linear dampening, is the Tip Undercut of the Straight Taper reed (Step 3.8.1), whereby the tip edge of the reed is made thinner from the inside by pulling sandpaper strips (on an angle) from between the blades as they are squeezed shut. This procedure can generally be used on any reed at any time to dampen *buzziness*. According to Skinner, Carl Mechler and some French reed makers used files to accomplish linear dampening.

Because linear enhancements work by sloping or "pyramiding" the fibers on the inside of the blade, they are most effectively used on a Straight Taper reed, which also functions with a slope or "pyramiding" of the fibers on the top side of the blade. In effect, a linearly enhanced Straight Taper reed has a "double pyramiding" effect, with slopes in opposite directions from the tip edge to the collar on both sides of the blade. Conversely, *flutes*—in which cane is removed from the inside of the blades parallel to the bark—theoretically work most effectively with a Tip Taper reed, where the outside of the blade from 43 mm to the collar is more parallel with the inside. In effect, a fluted Tip Taper reed has "double paralleling," at least on the back portion of the blades.

6.1.1 *LE 22 Reed*

Skinner most often used a 2-mm *brevis* with this variation, meaning that after the cane was shaped, he would remove 2 mm of cane from each butt end. The cane would then be 116 mm long, and the first pencil mark (given as 24 mm from the butt in Step 1 below) would now be 22 mm from the butt end. Hence, he named this linear-enhancement variation *LE 22*. The effect of the *brevis* was to utilize a wider part of the shaper, giving a reed with wider blades and tip edge.

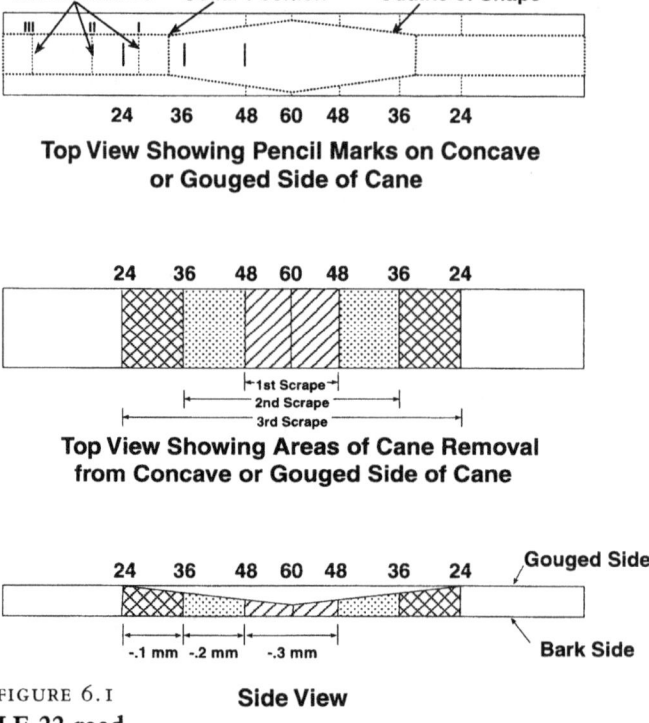

FIGURE 6.1
LE 22 reed

---

ening (HD) to be an external procedure that was done to the outside of the blades. All reeds receive HD to a certain extent, but not all reeds receive LD.

Method

Make these enchancements BEFORE Step 3.1.6 or 4.1.6, *Profiling*

Step 1: With a pencil compass, mark (on the inside of the cane) 24 mm, 36 mm, 48 mm, and 60 mm from each butt end.

Step 2: With a scraper that matches the inside curvature of the tube (#30, #32, or #36), scrape ten times in each direction between the 48-mm marks over the center. Reduce the thickness of the tube by 0.10 mm in the center.

NOTE: If you use a scraper which *matches* the inside curvature of the tube, less cane will be taken out of the area that will become the sides of the blades. Consequently, when profiled, the sides of the blades will be from softer cane, farther from the bark. If you use a scraper which slightly *exceeds* the inside curvature of the tube, more cane will be taken out of the area that will become the sides of the blades. Consequently, when profiled, the sides of the blades will be from harder cane, closer to the bark. Softer cane at the sides means that, in general, you will have to leave more cane in the mid-range and wings of the blades in Steps 3.5 and 4.5, "Parallel Sides Pre-Trim." Harder cane at the sides means that you can take out more cane in the mid-range and wings.

Step 3: Repeat the scraping (ten times in each direction) between the 36-mm marks, reducing the thickness of the cane between the 36-mm and 48-mm marks by 0.10 mm, and in the center (between the two 48-mm marks) by a total of 0.20 mm (including the reduction from Step 2).

Repeat the scraping (ten times in each direction) between the two 24-mm marks, reducing the thickness of the cane between the 24-mm and 36-mm marks by 0.10 mm; the area between the 36-mm and 48-mm marks by a total of 0.20 mm, and the center by a total of 0.30 mm.

Step 4: Smooth the inside of the entire tube with 220 WD. Proceed to Step 3.1.6 or 4.1.6, Profiling

Since Skinner presented this variation most often with a *brevis*, the pre-trim must be changed as follows:

3.2 or 4.2	*Pre-Trim*
3.2.1 or 4.2.1	*Smooth and polish inside of gouge with 400 WD.*
3.2.2 or 4.2.2	*Shape cane as described, then remove 2 mm from each butt end with a pair of sharp curved garden pruning shears. (This trimming is the* brevis.*)*
3.2.3 or 4.2.3	*Mark collar and wire positions as described.*
3.3 or 4.3	*OMIT enhancement of the inside of the tube.*

3.4 or 4.4   *Perform center-panel scoring as described.*

6.1.2 *LE 43-50 (Charleston or Loonie) variation*

A linear-enhancement effect smaller than the LE 22 can be achieved by starting the slope farther from the butt ends, and by taking out less cane. The result will be less pyramiding of fibers and, consequently, less resistance in the blades. The Charleston variation (Figure 6.2) was developed by Skinner and the author in 1986 on Charleston Lake (in the Rideau area of Ontario) while we listened to loons. In general, it illustrates how subtle linear enhancement can be, as opposed to the extensive cutting involved in making the LE 22. The increased resistance of the LE 22 reed, because of a greater pyramiding of fibers, will result in a darker sound with fewer high overtones and less of a tendency for the reed to *buzz*. The Charleston reed will be an easier-blowing reed with a lighter sound and more overtones. You can make a linear enhancement to suit your own needs.

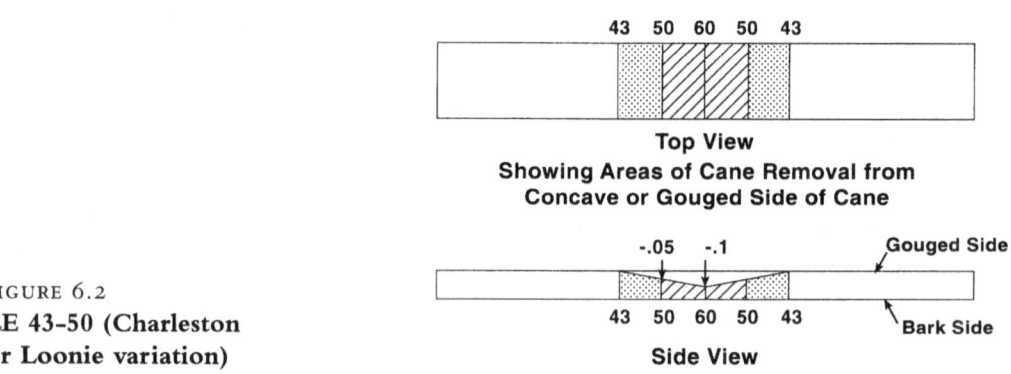

FIGURE 6.2
LE 43-50 (Charleston or Loonie variation)

Method

Make this enhancement BEFORE Step 3.1.6

Step 1: With a pencil compass, mark 43 mm and 50 mm from each butt end on the inside of the tube.

Step 2: With a scraper that matches the inside curvature of the cane, scrape three strokes in each direction between the two 50-mm mark. This should reduce the thickness of the cane by 0.05 mm in the center.

Step 3: Repeat scraping three times in each direction between the 43-mm marks. Reduce the thickness in this area by 0.05 mm, for a total reduction of 0.10 mm in the center.

Step 4: Smooth the inside of the entire tube with 220 WD.

NOTE: On a Straight Taper reed, this procedure, when combined with an Inside Tip Taper (Step 3.8.1), provides a reed with extremely flexible articulation and wide dynamic control. Proceed to Step 3.1.6. No *brevis* is required.

6.1.3 LE 22-45 variation

This variation, shown in Figure 6.3, is a linear enhancement designed to work with Tip Taper reeds, but it will also work with Straight Taper reeds. Basically, a slope is created on the inside of the cane from between wires II and III (22 mm from the butt end) to 45 mm, the point in the blades where the outside tip taper starts[29] (Figure 4.1, *Diagram of side view of straight and tip taper profiles on dry cane*). Between the 45-mm marks, across the center, the cane is parallel to the bark. This means that when the profile is applied, the tip edge of the reed will be taken from the cane slightly farther from the bark than it is in the LE 22 variation. Therefore, the tip of the LE 22-45 reed will be slightly softer than the tip of the LE 22 reed, and slightly harder than a Tip Taper reed with no linear enhancement. This reed is made with a 2-mm *brevis*.

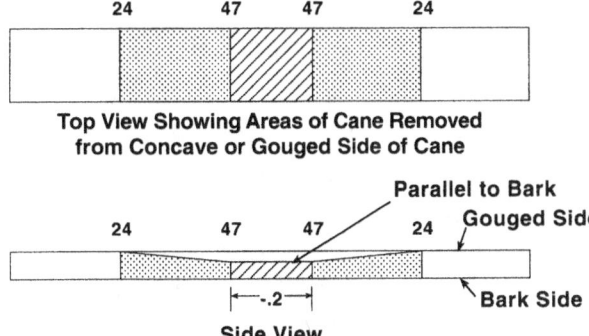

FIGURE 6.3
LE 22-45 variation

Method

Make this enhancement BEFORE Step 3.1.6 or 4.1.6

Step 1: With a pencil compass, mark 24 mm and 47 mm from the butt ends.

Step 2: With a scraper that matches the inside curvature of the cane, reduce the thickness of the cane between the two 47-mm marks by 0.20 mm (about 20 scrapes in each direction).

Step 3: Scrape from the 47-mm to 24-mm marks on both sides, decreasing the pressure of the scrape approaching the 24-mm mark. This should produce a slope with no reduction of cane thickness at all at the 24-mm mark to a 0.20 mm reduction of cane thickness at the 47-mm mark. The area between the 47-mm marks remains parallel to the bark, reduced 0.20 mm in thickness.

---

29. Skinner states that the Tip Taper profile should start at the 50-mm mark. However, he is referring to where the machined profile should start. By the time you have completed the final trim, you will have moved the slope (by hand, with sandpaper) back to approximately the 45-mm mark.

Step 4: Smooth out the inside of the cane and the transition points at 34 mm and 47 mm with 220 WD.

Since this variation requires a *brevis*, the pre-trim must be changed as follows:

3.2   Pre-Trim

3.2.1 or 4.2.1   Smooth and polish inside of gouge with 400 WD.

3.2.2 or 4.2.2   Shape cane as described, then remove 2 mm from each butt end with a sharp pair of curved garden pruning shears. (This trimming is the brevis.)

3.2.3 or 4.2.3   Mark collar and wire positions as described.

3.3 or 4.3   OMIT enhancement of the inside of the tube.

3.4 or 4.4   Center-Panel Scoring as described.

6.2 THE DIP TIP VARIATION

This variation is in a sense the opposite of the linear enhancements. In the linearly enhanced reeds, the inside slope runs from the tube (where the reed is thickest) to the tip edge (where it is thinnest). In the *Dip Tip*, the slope runs the other way, being thickest at the tip and thinner at the inside of the collar. Therefore, when this reed is profiled, the cane nearer to the collar will be cut closer to the bark and will therefore be harder than the cane nearer to the tip. The tip edge of this reed will *dip down* when formed and will give a very dampened or dark sound that will allow the player to achieve very soft dynamics, especially in the low register. Another way to understand this variation is to view it as an extension of the Reverse Corona (Section 5.2) into the blades. This reed should be made with the Tip Taper profile.

Method

4.1.5 Gouge cane.

The gouge needed for the Dip Tip is thicker than the gouge needed for the previous variations. Use a *mildly eccentric gouge* of 1.5 mm in the center and at least 1.25 mm at the edge, or use a *concentric gouge* of 1.5 mm.

4.1.6   OMIT profiling cane (see below).

4.1.7   Dry cane.

4.2   Pre-Trim

4.2.1   Smooth and polish inside of gouge with 400 WD.

4.2.2 Shape cane as described, then remove 2 mm from each butt end with a pair of curved garden pruning shears. (This trimming is the brevis.)

4.2.3 Mark collar and wire positions as described.

Step 1: With a pencil compass, mark 28 mm and 45 mm from each butt end.

Step 2: Using a scraper that matches the inside curvature of the tube, scrape gently along the shape on all four sides from the 45-mm mark toward the butt end. Stop the scrape at approximately 28 mm from the butt end (between the collar and wire I). Reduce the thickness of the cane by 0.25 mm.

Step 3: Remove the shoulders along the scrape in the blade area (blend the edge of the scrape into the blade area) with 220 WD.

Step 4: Profile cane as described in 4.1.6; cane can be profiled dry. Then proceed to Section 4.3, the Windsor Mill Process, which is required for the Dip Tip.

6.3 FLUTE GOUGE VARIATIONS

In these variations, shown in Figure 6.4, cane is taken out from inside of the gouged tube *parallel* to the bark and generally from the center of the tube. The result will be to increase the *eccentricity* of the gouge, making an eccentric gouge more elliptical and a concentric gouge more inverted.

Because the gouge of the reed is made thinner along the spine, *flutes* utilize harder cane in the spine of the reed. Since the cane is removed

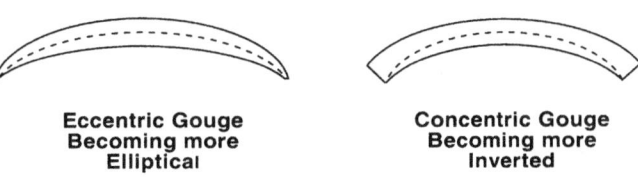

FIGURE 6.4 **Flute gouges**

parallel to the bark, there is no pyramiding of the fibers on the inside of the blades, and consequently no dampening effect. In general, *flutes* allow the blades to vibrate more freely. Skinner felt that fluted reeds gave the sound more direction and center. He sometimes referred to fluting as "resonance cuts" because fluting not only allows the blades to vibrate more freely, but the increase of space on the inside of the reed allows the player to use more air and consequently to achieve greater resonance in the sound. In this book, the term "resonance cuts" refers specifically to the removal of cane from the inside of the blades and parallel to the shape, as in the Vivaldi Reed (Section 6.3.3).

6.3.1 Center Flute with eccentric gouge

Because the procedure takes cane out of the tube parallel to the bark (the outer surface of the cane), this variation is most effectively used with the Tip Taper profile. Essentially, this procedure runs the entire length of the gouge. However, the inside radius in the tube areas (the area between the butt and the 30-mm mark) *matches* the outside radius of the cane (2.54 cm), while the inside radius of the scraping in the blade areas is *smaller* than the outside radius of the cane. *Do not begin by shaping the cane.*

Method

   4.2 Pre-Trim

      OMIT Step 4.2.1 (That is, do not smooth and polish inside of gouge at this point.)

      OMIT Step 4.2.2 (That is, do not shape the cane at this point.)

      Step 1: With a pencil compass, mark 30 mm and 22 mm from each butt end on the inside of the tube (Figure 6.5). Using a #16 or #20 scraper, reduce the thickness of the tube between the two 30-mm marks by 0.10 mm at the center (ten scrapes in each direction). Blend the scrapes over each 30-mm mark into the tube area, but no farther than 22 mm from the butt end.

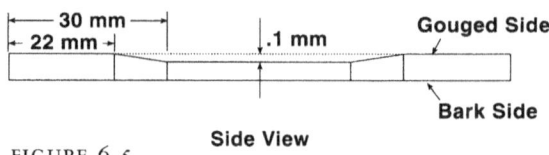

FIGURE 6.5
Side view of Step 6.3.1, *Center Flute with eccentric gouge* (Steps 1 and 2)

      Step 2: Remove shoulders of the scrape with #16 or #20 scraper or with 220 WD. Blend the scrape into the sides of the tube.

      Step 3: With a #32 scraper, reduce the thickness of the tube area (from the 30-mm mark to each butt end) by 0.10 mm.

      NOTE: This is essentially the Windsor Mill Process, so OMIT Section 3.2;

OR

      If you retain the flare on the shape (Step 6.1.1), a Reverse Corona (5.2) or Tube Taper (5.4) can replace the Windsor Mill.

   4.1.6 Profile cane.

   4.2.1 Smooth and polish inside of the gouge with 400 WD sandpaper.

   4.2.2 Shape cane.

   4.2.3 Mark collar and wire positions.

      GO TO Step 4.3.5

   6.3.2 *Center Flute with inverted gouge*

      By definition, if one uses cane with an inverted gouge, then one is using a Center Flute variation. The method is the same as 6.3.1 but with Steps 1 and 2 omit-ted. However, it is still necessary to return the tube area of the reed to a radius of 2.54 cm (Step 3) and to use a *Windsor Mill, Reverse Corona,* or *Tube Taper.*

6.3.3 *The Vivaldi reed (a variation of Center Flute)*

This reed has weaker sides and is more open on the inside than a Center Flute reed (Figure 6.6). Skinner felt that it gave the player the depth, resonance, and responsiveness necessary to play a Vivaldi concerto, and, for the book, he referred to this type of fluting as "resonance cuts." He also preferred the collar to be at 29 mm and the blades to be 27 mm long.

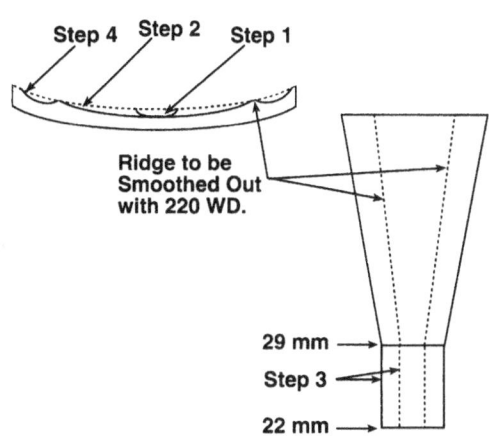

FIGURE 6.6
Cross-section of cane in center for Vivaldi variation and top view of resonance-cut ridges

Method

OMIT Step 4.2.1. (That is, do not smooth and polish inside of gouge at this point.)

4.2.2 *Shape cane*

Step 1: With a pencil compass, mark 30 mm and 22 mm from each butt end on the inside of the tube. With a #16 or #20 scraper, make a pilot cut down the middle between the two 22-mm marks, reducing the thickness of the cane by 0.15 mm or 0.20 mm (15 or 20 strokes in each direction). If the cane is hard, reduce the thickness by 0.25 mm or 0.30 mm.

Step 2: Make a pencil mark down the length of the pilot cut. With a #28 scraper, remove cane between the two 30-mm marks until the pencil mark disappears.

Step 3: With a #24 scraper, smooth out the transition from 30 mm to 22 mm. Sand with 220 WD.

Step 4: With a #16 or #20 scraper, add resonance cuts to a depth of 0.10 mm around the bahn (parallel to the sides of the shape) and into the tube area. Smooth out the ridge of the resonance cuts with 220 WD.

4.1.6 *Profile cane.*

6.3.4   *Flat or elliptical flute*

Skinner preferred to use the Straight Taper reed for this variation. ***Do not profile cane yet.***

Method

> OMIT Step 3.2.1 (That is, do not smooth and polish inside of gouge at this point.)

3.2.2   *Shape cane*

> **Step 1:** With a #16 scraper, reduce the thickness of the cane by 0.10 mm from butt to butt in two straight ribbons, so that the outside of each ribbon touches the shape at its narrowest point (Figure 6.7).
>
> **Step 2:** Between the two 30-mm marks, remove the bump in the middle of the cane with 220 WD until the center of the cane is flat.

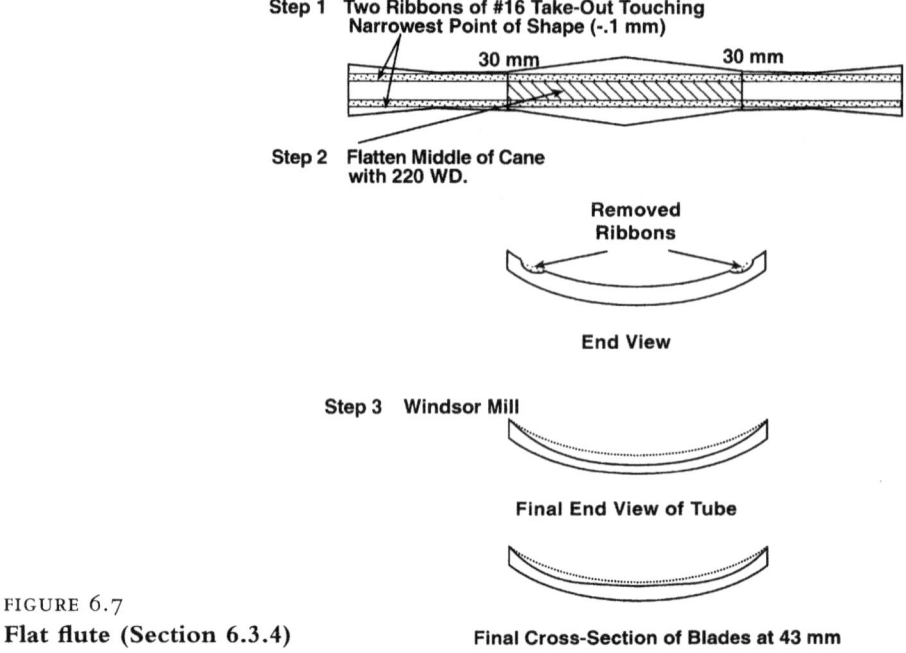

FIGURE 6.7
Flat flute (Section 6.3.4)

> **Step 3:** Return the tube area to a radius of 2.54 cm with the Windsor Mill Process (Section 3.3).

3.1.6   *Profile cane.*

6.4   THE SANDBOARD REED

The purpose of this variation, according to Skinner, was to put the wings and the flare at the butt ***all in the same plane***. The result is to make the sides of the blades very thin from the inside of the reed. The *Sandboard* reed variation, shown in Figure 6.8, is best used with a Tip Taper profile and an eccentric gouge. Skinner thought that Knochenhauer and Del Negro did this on most of their reeds.

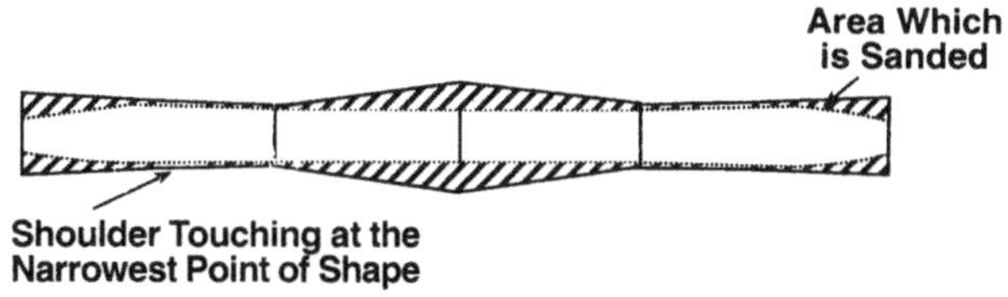

FIGURE 6.8
Top view of gouge for Sandboard reed

Method

4.2.2 Shape cane.

Step 1: Put a piece of 200 DRY or 220 WD sandpaper at least 15 cm square on a flat surface. Hold the cane gouged-side down so that one butt and the center of the cane are flat on the surface. The other end will be slightly elevated. Sand the butt and wing so that the shoulders created on the sides of the gouge touch each other at the narrowest point of the shape. Repeat on the other side.

Step 2: With a #32 scraper, remove the border of the shoulder from the full length of the cane, and restore the tube area to 2.54 cm radius (this replaces the Windsor Mill Process);

OR

With a #24 scraper, remove the border of the shoulder in the blade area parallel to the shape (Section 6.5 on EDAS as follows).

4.1.6 Profile cane.

NOTE: For this reed, Skinner recommended keeping the flare on the shape and doing a bevel on the tube (Section 5.5 *Beveling Variation*).

6.5 EVEN DOWN ABOUT SHAPE (EDAS)

This is a variation that could be applied to almost any Tip Taper reed. By opening up the inside of the blades, it effectively undampens the sound. This variation is a simpler version of the *1001 Sheherezade* reed described later (in Section 8.3). The radius of the scraper affects the sound of the reed. Basically, the larger the scraper, the more the highs in the reed will be emphasized.

Method

4.2.2 Shape cane.

Step 1: With a pencil compass, mark 30 mm from each butt end. With a #24 (or larger) scraper, reduce the thickness of the cane parallel to the shape from the center to just beyond the 30-mm mark.

Step 2: Remove the shoulders of the scrape with 220 WD.

4.1.6 Profile cane.

NOTE: Skinner preferred to keep the flare on this reed and to use a Reverse Corona or a Tube Taper.

CHAPTER 7

VARIATIONS TO THE OUTSIDE OF THE BLADES

Picking up where Chapters 3 and 4 left off, this chapter addresses two processes that take place simultaneously: *voicing* and *trouble shooting*. In the following, Skinner starts the "final stage" (Sections 3.7 and 4.7) of basic reed construction. As in the earlier chapters, direct quotations from Lou Skinner appear in **boldface** here and are taken from audio tapes that the author and Skinner made in the summer of 1990.

All reeds need an outside and an inside trim. After thoroughly drying the reed, I retighten the wires. Then I take the tip edge down to 0.25 mm with the plaque in. Then I take the plaque out and take the wings down over the tip edge. Then I dampen it to remove cane from the spine as much as it needs from the collar to 43 mm (Steps 3.8.2 and 4.8.2). I check the peep first to see what it needs. This is called *tuning* the reed. I consider this to be the final peep. If I need to dampen the reed more, I take out cane from the very edge of the reed from the collar to 23 mm (53 mm from the butt or 3 mm from the tip edge). This drops the lows and makes them have a *direct sound*.

For the inside trim, I start by pulling sandpaper once in the middle of the tip edge and once obliquely on either side (Step 3.8.1, *Tip Undercut*). Then, if you want to dampen more, or if you want to make the sides more flexible, do it from 43 mm to the tip edge.

The only time that you touch the backbone is if the peep is too high. When you do the inside trim you raise the upper crow. The outside trim darkens or dampens the reed.

7.1 APERTURE

From this point onward, our concern will be with how the reed vibrates, so it would be useful to recall the discussion of apertures in Chapter 1. Aperture requirements vary tremendously from player to player and from reed to reed, but all apertures must be able to vibrate. Therefore, the size of the opening, the thickness of the tip edge, and the dampening of the center as compared to the sides must be of acceptable dimensions.

7.1.1   *Aperture size*

The center of the blades should be between 1.5 mm and 2.5 mm apart. Adjust the opening if necessary by changing wire I; flattening wire I (by squeezing on the top and bottom) will close the aperture, and opening wire I (by squeezing on the sides) will open the aperture.

7.1.2   *Tip-edge thickness*

The thickness of the tip edge of the blades should be around 0.25 mm across the whole reed. If you need to make the tip edge thinner, insert the metal plaque and use either 220, 320, or 400 WD or the sapphire file over the tip edge (Figure 3.9).

7.1.3   *Aperture dampening*

The aperture should be partially dampened. (Refer to Chapter 1, Figure 1.2, *Aperture of Reeds*.)

7.2   VOICING

With the term *voicing*, Skinner referred to two aspects of the reed: the actual pitches of the crow (tuning) and the color of the sound that the reed produced on the instrument (resonance and presence). Skinner tuned the pitches of the crow to the natural pitches that the reed should produce according to the blade and bahn lengths. He adjusted the height of wire I primarily to control the color of the sound, and to a lesser extent to control the pitches of the reed. Since the position of wire I determines the bahn length and therefore the low pitch of the reed, Skinner borrowed for wire I the name "capo d'astro" from guitar terminology. The "capo d'astro" is the metal bar which fits across the strings on the neck of the guitar and slides up and down to change the pitch of the strings. Likewise, the closer that wire I is placed to the tip edge, the higher the low pitch of the reed; the farther, the lower.

7.2.1   *Tuning the reed*

Reed pitch was discussed in Chapter 1. To review, the crow is made up of three pitches: a low pitch, a mid-range pitch an octave above the low pitch, and an even-higher pitch. Assuming that the finished reed is 55 mm to 56 mm in overall length, with a tip 14.5 mm to 15.5 mm wide, and a collar width of 8 mm to 8.75 mm, the *natural pitches* of the reed crow should be as shown in Table 7.1. (This table is extracted from Table 1.1.)

TABLE 7.1 **Natural pitches of reed crows, based on blade and bahn lengths**

Natural High Pitch of Reed		Natural Low Pitch of Reed	
Blade Length	*Pitch*	*Bahn Length*	*Pitch*
25 mm	F	31 mm	B
26 mm	E	30 mm	C
27 mm	E flat	29 mm	C sharp
28 mm	D	28 mm	D
29 mm	C sharp	27 mm	E flat

Thus, the Straight Taper and Tip Taper reeds described in Chapters 3 and 4 were referred to by Skinner as *C models* because the low pitch is C based on a bahn length of 30 mm. The high pitch is E natural, based on a blade length of 26 mm. Since the high pitch **is controlled by the length of the backbone . . . and by the density of the cane in the backbone . . . and is the most stable** of the reed pitches, it is necessary to *tune* this pitch, especially if it is sharper than what its *natural pitch* should be.

7.2.1.a   *Method of tuning reed pitches*

The following steps are supplemental to those of Chapters 3 and 4.

a) Consulting Table 7.1, determine what the high pitch, or "peep," of the reed should be.

b) Peep the reed.

Peeping means that you produce only the high pitch of the reed, which is accomplished by placing your embouchure at the collar or over wire I. Start blowing very gently, keeping your embouchure pressure at a minimum, and do not try to get a sound yet. Increase your air pressure gradually until the reed makes a soft sustainable high pitch. That sound will be the high pitch of the reed, or the "peep."

c) Tune the peep to the natural pitch if required.

If the peep is at the natural pitch determined by your blade length, do nothing. If the peep is above the natural pitch, check to see if the aperture is too closed. If it is, open it by inserting a pin mandrel (usually #9), or by squeezing wire I on the sides of the reed. You can also scrape cane out of the backbone and on the sides of the reed (from 5 mm in front of the collar to the 43-mm mark) until the correct pitch is reached. If the peep is below the natural pitch, you may have removed too much cane from the backbone or from the heart areas. At this point you can decide to do nothing (especially if the discrepancy is a tone or less), or you can try to raise the pitch of the peep by closing the aperture at wire I, or by repeating the Tip Undercut (Step 3.8.1), or by making the reed shorter, taking tiny amounts of cane off the tip edge until the crow is raised.

d) Tune the lows.

Isolating the lows from the high pitch requires practice. Try to force the reed to play only the lows by placing your embouchure at the collar, dropping your jaw (to enlarge the mouth cavity as much as possible), and opening your throat as much as possible as you blow forcefully.

The low natural pitches of the reed are less stable than the high pitch, and less critical for reed-tuning purposes. However, if the low pitches are too high, check to see if the cane is too thick in the heart area (the center and mid-ranges between 43 mm and 50 mm). If those thicknesses are correct, you can drop the low pitches by removing cane along 5 mm to 8 mm of the spine directly in front of the collar, about 3 to 4 mm wide. Under the light, it will appear that you have created a window in the spine. If the low natural pitches are too low and if the reed plays too flat on your instrument, the only solution will be to clip back the tip, thus shortening the blade and bahn lengths, as well as the whole reed.

If the reed generally plays all right on your instrument but is a bit flat, or the open F or one-finger E falls, remember that as you play the reed, the fibers will gradually fill up with fluids from your breath and become a bit harder, and those problems might disappear in a few days. If not, then the only thing to do is to clip back the tip.

7.2.2 *Adjusting the resonance of the reed: the rounded tube vs. the oval tube and the concept of presence in the sound*

In addition to tuning the reed by removing cane from the blades or by undercutting or clipping the tip, the pitch and resonance of the reed are controlled by *wire I* and by the *shape of the tube*.

A *rounder* tube at wire I produces a *deeper* inside, or more air space on the inside of the blades, which in turn permits a greater amplitude of vibration. It will also *lower* the pitch of the reed (including its partials), as well as *covering* or dampening the sound when played on the bassoon. Skinner pointed out that to compensate for the increase in resistance that a rounder wire I causes, it was necessary to take cane out of the spine from the collar to the 43-mm mark. He referred to the sound produced by a rounded wire I as **darker, as if the sound *presence* were inside the *reed*.**

The *oval* shaped tube, vertically flattened at wire I, is more *shallow* and therefore does not permit the amplitude of vibration that a more rounded wire I allows; it does permit the pitches or partials of the reed to be more *natural*. Skinner referred to the sound on the bassoon as **having *presence*.... The sound will seem as if it were on the outside of the *instrument*.**

The more oval wire I or the **shallower the tube**, the more *open*, outside, and *present* the sound will be. It will have carrying power. The more rounded wire I, the more *covered* and inside the sound will be.

7.2.3 *Presence and the differences between Mechler and Knochenhauer reeds*

Presence . . . the sound is outside the instrument. It carries, and if you are close to the player, it seems as if the sound is outside the instrument. That's the way the Carl Mechler reed worked. So, we said it had *presence*, and, of course, it has an oval throat, and a small throat (Chapter 9). . . . A reed that is built round and wide at the first wire has a sound that stays in the instrument. If there are no other instruments playing, you hear it very well, but if there are any other instruments playing, it does not cut through those other *instrumental* voices. Therefore, it does not have *presence*.

Some of Carl Mechler's reeds had a natural high pitch of E flat, but they had an oval throat. The Carl Mechler reed had a *dark* sound with presence. Now, what constitutes *darkness*? *Dampening constitutes darkness*. For our purposes, we are looking for a bassoon with an *heroic* sound (referring to John Miller's sound) . . . it cuts through and it is dark. It is dark because the reed is dampened on the sides. Carl Mechler reeds were heavy on the sides and dampened at the tip, and yet they carried through the orchestra because they had an oval throat.

A reed heavy on the sides with nothing done to the tip will *buzz*. The sides will rattle against each other *producing the buzz*. Dampening at the tip (Chapter 1, Figure 1.2 and Step 3.8.1, *Tip Undercut*) will give you a bit more resistance. A reed that is too *loose* or too easy to play will allow you to *over tongue*. An undampened reed will allow you to tongue faster than the reed is able to articulate.

With wire I too rounded, the blades are too arched, and this results in a compression of the fibers on the inside of the cane in the mid range and high range. This can be relieved by taking cane out of the spine. If you make the spine and sides of an arched reed **thinner**, you will decrease the aperture size. But that kind of a reed does not carry as well as a reed with an oval first wire.

Sound outside the reed means *presence*. It means that the first overtone is stronger. That formant[30] is for color. But *presence* is when the overtone or *shadow note*, is strong. When you hear a good bassoonist, you hear two sounds, the fundamental and the second octave. Therefore, low F has a *shadow* one octave up. Also, the one-finger E has the octave above as a *shadow tone*. That gives the sound *presence*. If a *reed* has three sounds, it will have *presence*.

The Carl Mechler reed has *presence*, and the Knochenhauer does not. The Knochenhauer reed is dead compared to the Carl Mechler. The Knochenhauer reed is arched higher, so Sol Schoenbach cut the back out to make it play easier. The Knochenhauer stays in the horn and is *darker*.

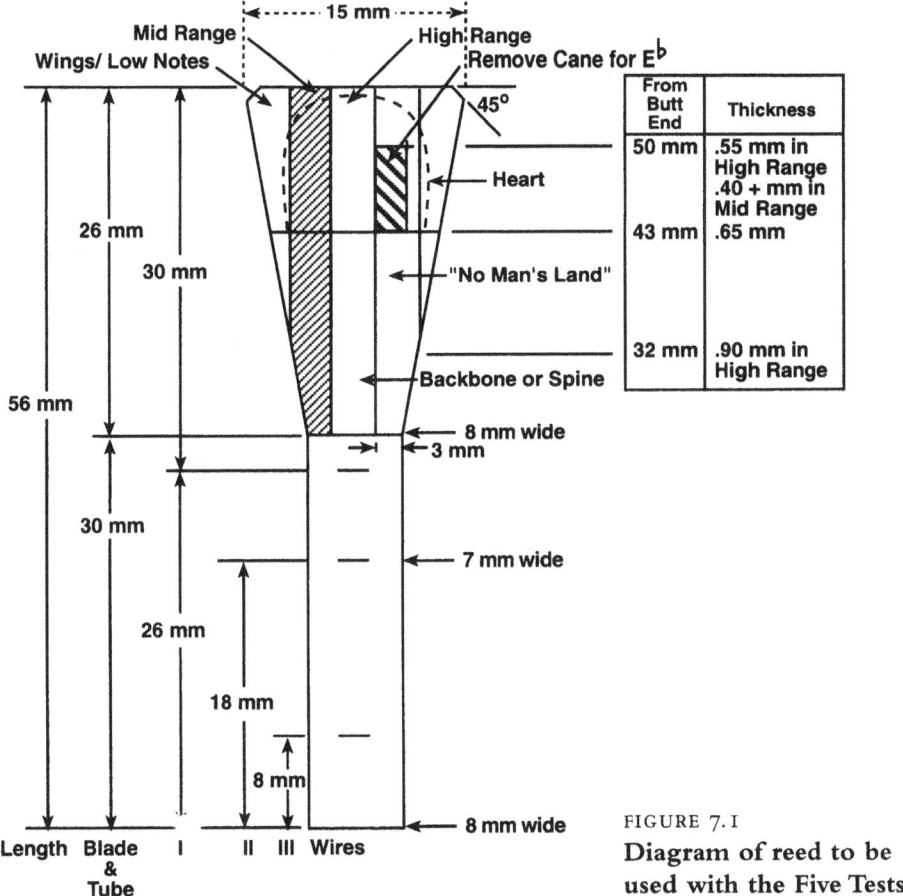

FIGURE 7.1
Diagram of reed to be used with the Five Tests

7.3 TROUBLESHOOTING: THE FIVE TESTS

These tests were developed by Skinner and the author for the 1986 York University seminar. Further work was done in the summer of 1990, and Skinner requested they be included in the book. The following tables are to be used in conjunction with the tests and with Figure 7.1.

NOTE: It is best to perform all five tests before taking the corrective steps recommended in Tables 7.2 through 7.5.

Test 1 Low F_1

Low F_1 should play freely and should feel as if you could make an infinite crescendo on it. It should not collapse when pushed.

30. Skinner is referring to the first overtone of the bassoon as a formant. Strictly speaking, formants on the bassoon are not necessarily the first overtone. For example, the formant for low F_1 is the second overtone, or middle C. Nonetheless, he makes a valid point about the importance and strength of overtones, especially the first two, in establishing sound color.

TABLE 7.2 **Test 1, Tests for overall balance of cane in the blades**

PROBLEM	CHECK FOR	SOLUTION
Low F_1 is stuffy	Aperture too open	Close aperture at wire I so that center opening is 2 mm or less.
	Tip edge too thick	Take tip edge down with sandpaper and plaque (Steps 3.8.2 and 4.8.2) or with knife or sapphire file.
	Too much cane in heart	Thickness should be about 0.65 mm at 43 mm and 0.55 mm at 50 mm. Remove cane with knife or 220 WD.
Low F_1 collapses	Too much cane out of heart	Usually thickness at 50 mm has dropped below 0.50 mm. Clip 0.05 mm off tip.
Low F_1 is too buzzy	Cane is too heavy in the wing areas	Take cane out from 43 mm to tip edge on upper sides of blades.
	Tip edge is too heavy	Tip edge should be 0.25 mm thick. Repeat 3.8.1, *Tip Undercut*.

Test 2 Open F and E

Find out how much over-blowing and jaw-dropping you need to *force* an open F and one-finger E down a semi-tone.

TABLE 7.3 **Test 2, Tests for cane in the heart, especially at the 50-mm mark**

PROBLEM	CHECK FOR	SOLUTION
Open F and/or one-finger E can be forced down only with difficulty, and can be played within a comfortable dynamic range without falling	No problem	You have the right amount of cane in the heart: about 0.65 mm thickness at 43 mm and about 0.55 mm thickness at 50 mm.
Open F and E fall too easily in pitch when played	Thickness of cane at 50 mm	You have probably taken out too much cane at 50 mm (>0.50 mm). Clip 0.05 mm off tip and try again. Keep clipping tip until F and E stabilize.
Open F and E cannot be forced down in pitch	Too much cane in the heart	Bring the thickness of the blades at 43 mm to 0.65 mm and at 50 mm to 0.55 mm.

Test 3 Forked E flat

Play forked E flat from ff and decrescendo to pp. Do not use a right-hand block (addition of B flat and index or middle finger — or low E flat key). The note should be stable and should not *shoot up* in pitch when blown hard and when making a diminuendo.

TABLE 7.4 **Test 3, Tests for cane in the mid-range section of the heart (either side of center, just behind the tip) in the 43- to 50-mm part of the blades**

PROBLEM	CHECK FOR	SOLUTION
Forked E flat shoots up in pitch at loud dynamics and when making a diminuendo (similar problem with the B flat immediately above)	There is too much cane in the area indicated on Figure 7.1	Remove cane with knife or 220 WD from the area indicated on Figure 7.1. Make sure to *blend* your strokes into the wing and high-range areas, and into the tip area.
Forked E flat and D flat fall	You have taken out too much cane in the area indicated.	Either clip the tip or remove cane from the high-range area between 43 and 50 mm so that the relative thicknesses of the center (high-range) and mid-range areas are closer to each other.

Tests 4 and 5 Upper-register tonguing and low E1 and B2 attacked pp

You should be able to tongue vigorously in the high register and, at the same time, tongue *pp* in the low register.

Test 4

Tongue four sixteenth notes on high g, and repeat, moving chromatically upward to and beyond high c^1, and

Test 5

Attack low E1 and B1 *pp*.

TABLE 7.5 **Tests 4 and 5, Test for thickness across the tip edge and how the front 6 mm of the blades blend into the heart area (the solution will always be a compromise)**

PROBLEM	CHECK FOR	SOLUTION
You can tongue the high register but cannot attack low E1 and B2 *pp*	Thickness of tip edge	Your tip edge is too thick. Reduce thickness with knife and plaque or with 220 WD as in Steps 3.8.2 and 4.8.2. If your reed is also buzzy, then repeat Step 3.8.1, *Tip Undercut*. Blend your knife work into the area between the tip edge and the heart.
You can attack low E1 and B2 *pp*, but the reed collapses when you try to tongue in the high register	Thickness of tip edge	Your tip edge is too thin. Clip your tip edge until you can tongue in the high register, but not so much that you lose the ability to attack low E and B *pp*.

7.4 ADDITIONAL TROUBLESHOOTING

7.4.1 *Popping the corners*

Sometimes a reed will perform the Five Tests adequately but will not articulate easily enough in the low register. Skinner recommended "popping the corners" of the reed to open the aperture in the wing areas. If the aperture in the wing areas is too closed, then the aperture is effectively "half opened" without any embouchure pressure, according to Figure 1.2, "Aperture of Reeds." The solution is to open the aperture in the wing areas by gently flattening or squeezing the tube with pliers (preferably parallel-jaw pliers) between wires II and III until the corners of the reed "pop open" 0.1 mm. Hold this position for 5 seconds before releasing the pliers. The "adjustment notches" that you added in Step 3.6.14 or 4.6.14 are there to help the tube retain its new shape. This procedure improves low-register articulation with very little effect on the other characteristics of the reed.

NOTE: You can also make wire II more oval from top to bottom to "pop the corners," but this will drastically affect the other characteristics of the reed.

7.4.2 *Improving low D_1*

If low D_1 seems to be "stuffy," try removing a small amount of cane from the back of the wing areas on the sides of the blades. With your thumb and index finger on the edge of the blades, feel where the fibers tend to pyramid, and then reduce the thickness at that point.

CHAPTER 8

SPECIAL REEDS AND PROCESSES[31]

Those of us who studied with Skinner know that for the first few lessons he would show us a specific model of reed—such as the Straight Taper or Tip Taper, the Vivaldi, 1001, or 2001—from beginning to end. Over the years, he invented and taught literally hundreds of different reed models. In the discussions leading to this book, he decided that the most simple approach would be to describe two basic models with variations, as in musical themes and variations. Nevertheless, he also thought we should show the following *complete* reeds, although they are combinations of variations covered in Chapters 5, 6, and 7 applied to the basic Straight Taper or Tip Taper reeds explained in Chapters 3 and 4.

In his own collection of reeds from other makers, Skinner had samples from over fifty people, including Ferdinand Del Negro. Skinner's Del Negro reed model, however, is *not* a copy of the reeds that Del Negro made. Rather, it is Skinner's interpretation and his tribute to Del Negro's importance as a player, teacher, and reed maker. Likewise, Skinner often referred to the Straight Taper reed of Chapter 3 as the Walt Model—an hommage to Sherman Walt. A reed actually made by Sherman Walt and one by Ferdinand Del Negro are analyzed in Chapter 9.

8.1 THE DEL NEGRO MODEL

Skinner's *Del Negro* model reed borrows some of the principles of reed making used by Del Negro and by Knochenhauer, and it is built onto the Tip Taper reed described in Chapter 4.

---

31. In Chapters 5, 6, and 8, the variation or reed model is first discussed and then presented as a method. The numbers in italics refer to the relevant steps in Chapters 3 and 4. The first number refers to the chapter. The steps of the method are designed to replace those steps described in Chapters 3 and 4.

Because the Del Negro reed has a bahn length of 27 mm, the natural low pitch is E flat, and it is therefore necessary to lower the E flat to C. This is achieved by taking cane out of the sides, between the 43 mm mark and the collar, actually making the sides *knife-edge* thin, a technique and expression that Skinner attributed to Del Negro.

> *4.6.23 Put wire I on loosely between wire II and collar. Slide it and secure it 27 mm from the tip edge.*
>
> *4.6.24 Continue as described in Chapter 4.*
>
> *4.8.1 With 220 WD, remove cane along the sides, between the 43 mm mark to the collar, making the sides knife-edge thin.*
> *Make sure that the cane taken out is blended at least 3 mm into the spine. Continue as described.*

NOTE: This process can be repeated after the *final trim*, when the reed is wet, by scraping along the sides with a knife (held vertically to the blades) back and forth between the 43 mm mark and the collar. Enough cane has been removed when the lows of the crow reach C natural, or whichever natural pitch is desired. Remember also that in the Tip Taper reed, wire I can be made *rounder* or more arched, a process that will dampen the sound and will also drop the natural pitches of the entire reed.

8.2 OFFSET SHAPE

The idea behind this shape is to eliminate the need to side-slip the butt of the reed just after folding it over (Steps 3.6.2 and 4.6.2). Skinner cautioned, however, that it is not wise to do the Offset Shape if you are going to do any inside trim or enhancement of gouge, since it is obviously too difficult to offset the scraper wheels each time they cross the center line. For the same reasons, machine profiling can be problematic unless you use a thicker profile and compensate for the offset in the final trim.

> *3.2.2 and 4.2.2 Shape cane as described here.*
>
> **Step 1:** With a Fox #2 shaper, shape both quadrants of the reed on one end. Loosen the shaper and move the piece of cane over 0.50 mm so that when the other quadrants are shaped, the overall width of the reed will be 0.50 mm wider than the Fox #2 shaper.
>
> NOTE: You can also start the shape with a Fox #3 shaper and obtain the same result, but you must continue with a Fox #2 from this point.
>
> In Steps 3.6.2 and 4.6.2, the top blade is shifted or offset to the left about 1 mm or 2 mm. Since we want to obtain the same effect, we need to take off diagonally opposite quadrants of the shape.
>
> **Step 2:** Place the piece of cane back in the shaper. Holding the shaper convex side up, align the right side of the cane with the right side of the shaper.

Step 3: Remove the cane from the lower left quadrant.

Step 4: Slide the cane to the right so that the lower left quadrant is buried inside the shaper, and the upper left quadrant is matched to the shaper. Remove the cane from the upper right quadrant.

The shape should appear as in Figure 8.1, so that when it is folded over, the upper blade will be side-slipped to the left approximately 0.50 mm.

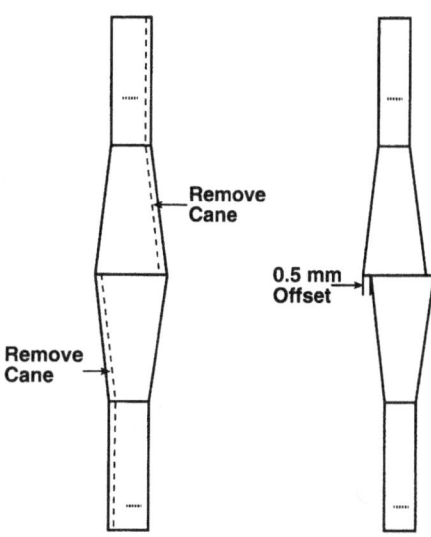

FIGURE 8.1 **Offset shaping**

8.3 THE 1001 SHEHEREZADE REED

Skinner referred to this reed as **a radical version of the EDAS process.** The *Even Down Around Shape* process (Section 6.5) basically created the trim on the *inside* of the blades instead of the outside. Skinner also described this reed as **self-trimming with very little to do to the outside** of the blades in the pre-trim. This reed is best used with a Tip Taper profile and can have a 2-mm *brevis*. Skinner thought that Del Negro used this inside trim to create a knife edge running from the collar to three-quarters of the way up the blades; for this he would use a small scraper and sandpaper.

4.1.6   Profile a Tip Taper as in Figure 4.1.

4.1.7   Dry cane on doweling.

OMIT Step 4.2.1 (That is, do not smooth and polish inside of gouge at this point.)

4.2.2   Shape cane

Step 1: With a sapphire file, file across the edges of the shape, as in Figure 8.2, establishing four flats on the shape. Continue thinning the edges of the cane until **a shelf... just over 1 mm wide appears around the entire shape. The sides must be thin enough to be playable.**

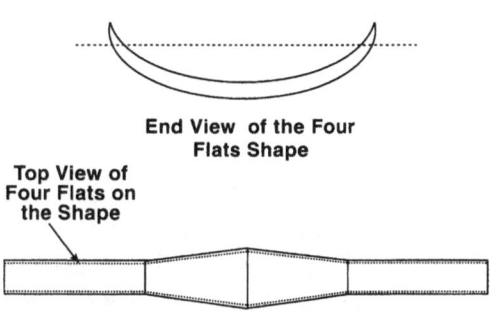

FIGURE 8.2 **Four Flats on the shape**

Step 2: The shoulder or inside edge of the shelf is removed by blending it into the gouge with a #28, #30, or #32 wheel (see Figure 8.3). Establish a radius of 28/32 by going up to—but not beyond—the outside edge of the reed. Be especially careful in the wing area: 43 mm to the centerfold. The cane here is very thin. Four or five sweeps with the wheel from 43 mm to the butt on each of the quadrants should be sufficient. Also, from 43 mm to the center, be careful not to extend the new radius into the mid-range area of the blades. This internal trim process is designed to take down the wing areas and the sides of the shape from the inside.

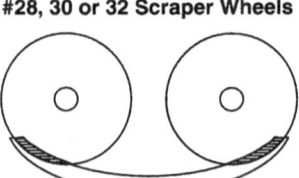

FIGURE 8.3
Removing the shoulder

Step 3: Smooth with 220 WD.

NOTE: In this process, if you are not completely comfortable with handling the scraper wheels, 220 WD is also effective, albeit slower.

4.1.6 *Profile cane.*

4.2 Pre-Trim

4.2.1. *Smooth and polish inside of gouge with 400 WD.*

OMIT Step 4.2.2 (Cane has already been shaped.)

4.2.3 *Mark collar and wire positions.*

4.3 *Enhancement of the Inside of the Tube*

Proceed to Section 5.3, *Four Flats with Take-Out,* for butt enhancement instead of the *Windsor Mill Process.*

4.4 *Center-Panel Scoring*

Proceed as described in Chapter 4.

4.5 *Parallel-Sides Pre-Trim*

OMIT Steps 4.5.1 to 4.5.4

4.5.5 *Sand entire surface lightly with 120 DRY.*

OMIT Steps 4.5.6 to 4.5.8

4.5.9 *Re-establish fold line with knife-edge file.*

NOTE: Depending on the profile, it may be necessary to take cane out of the blades 5 mm on either side of the fold (3 mm if a *brevis* was used) to allow the cane to be folded. Check the cane under a lamp; thickness at the fold line should be no greater than 0.40 mm.

4.5.10   Proceed as in Chapter 4.

NOTE: In the final trim of the 1001 reed, Skinner made sure that the spine at the collar was 0.80 mm thick and that the spine should remain that thick until the tip taper started, at 45 mm from the butt end. He would **do the center first, then . . . make the sides match the center.**

8.4   THE 2001 SPACE ODDITY REED

This reed is a Center Flute variation with an Inverted Gouge in the blades. It is built on a Straight Taper profile.

Method (*Do not profile or shape the cane yet.*)

3.3 Enhancement of the Gouge

Step 1: On the inside of the gouge, mark 30 mm from each butt end with a pencil compass. With a #24 scraper, scrape a center flute channel (Step 6.3.1) between the two 30-mm marks. The depth of the center flute—the amount cane removed—should be 0.10 mm (10 strokes in each direction should be sufficient).

Step 2: Take out the shoulder of the cut by blending it into the gouge with the #24 wheel or with 220 WD. Check the blades under the lamp to make sure that the cane is one color, indicating that the shoulders have been blended evenly into the gouge. The gouge of the blades is now mildly inverted.

NOTE: If you begin with a mildly inverted gouged piece of cane, you can omit Steps 1 and 2 above.

Step 3: Profile and shape cane as in Step 3.1.6 and Step 3.2.2.

Step 4: Make collar and wire marks: the collar is at 29 mm, and the wires at 8 mm and 18 mm (as in Step 3.2.3).

Step 5: Add a *Reverse Corona* to the tubes *(Section 5.2).*

Proceed to *3.4 Center-Panel Scoring.*

3.8 Final Trim

3.8.1   OMIT Tip Undercut at this time. This procedure can be done after the reed has been soaked and crowed if the tip needs to be dampened.

3.8.2   Blades

Step 1: Reduce the tip edge ONLY 2 mm back, not to the 43-mm mark. Use the metal plaque and 220 WD or a sapphire file.

Step 2: Make the edge of the reed knife-edge thin back to the 43-mm mark, but do not extend the knife edge from the 43-mm mark to the collar.

NOTE: Cane can be taken out from the 43-mm mark to the collar after the reed has been soaked and crowed. If the reed needs dampening, cane can be removed from the sides. If the highs need freeing up, cane can be removed from the spine.

Steps 3 to 7 as in Chapter 3.

Proceed to 3.8.3 and 3.8.4.

8.5 REGULAR OBOE TRIM

Until this point in the book, all of the reeds—whether Straight Taper, Tip Taper, or a hybrid of the two—had what Skinner referred to as a *thumbnail trim*, a heavier heart rounded at the corners. However, besides making bassoon reeds out of oboe cane, Skinner also borrowed two trims from the oboe reed.

a) Start with cane 1 mm thick.

b) Put a parallel profile on the cane from collar to collar (30 mm) to a thickness of 0.85 mm, or until the bark is gone. From a point 44 mm from the butt ends, profile a tip taper down to a thickness of 0.40 mm at the center.

c) The overall length of the reed is 58 mm, as in Figure 8.4.

d) The reed is trimmed as in Figure 8.4. Key notes (as indicated on the diagram) are low D, B flat, and forked E flat.

  * If the reed is too sharp or too hard, remove cane from the edge of the parallel trim.
  * Trimming the sides and corners just behind the tip (creating a minor *thumb nail*) will let you control pitch.

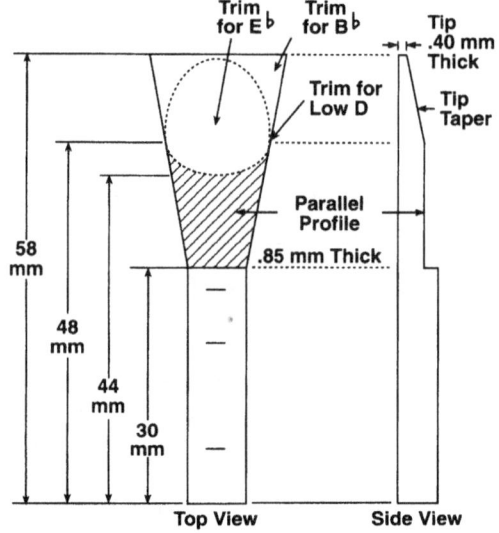

FIGURE 8.4 **Regular oboe trim**

8.6 THE TABUTEAU TRIM

a) The reed is 56 mm long, and the collar is in the middle at 28 mm. Use a Tip Taper profile.

b) A wider shape is needed: either a Fox #3, or a Fox #2 with off-set shaping, so the width of the tube at wire I is 12 mm or 12.5 mm. A convex Bavarian shape is also a good choice for this reed. The tip should be 15 mm to 15.5 mm wide.

c) The heart of the reed from 43 mm to 50 mm is left heavy.

* The tube at wire I is rounded, and the spine from 43 mm to the collar is scraped out to compensate for the roundness of wire I.
* The sides are thin.
* If the reed is too *dumpf*, you take out more cane from the heart. It is a Horizontally Dampened reed (it dampens from side to side) so high notes are from the middle and lows are from the entire tip edge.

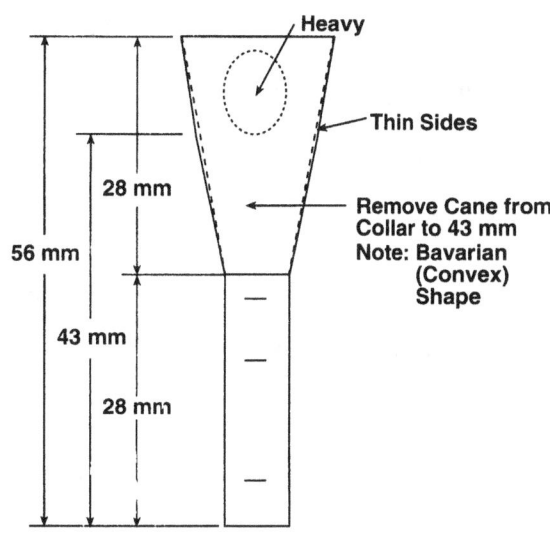

FIGURE 8.5 **Tabuteau trim**

8.7 KEEPING THE FLARE ON THE SHAPE

The difference in keeping the flare on the shape and removing it is seen and felt in the aperture. If the flare is removed (as in Chapters 3 and 4), the sides of the tube can be pulled closer together. Using wire II as a fulcrum, the result is that the pressure on the aperture will be to open it. If the flare is kept on the shape, using wire II as a fulcrum, the resulting pressure on the aperture will tend to close it. You can use either approach with any reed style, depending on whether you want the aperture to be pressured open or closed. This procedure is very compatible with the Tube Taper variation (Section 5.4). For steps that are identical to the similar steps in Chapters 3 and 4, only the titles will be used here. The reader can refer to the earlier chapters for details.

3.6 or 4.6	***Forming and Drying***
3.6.1 or 4.6.1	*Fold cane but DO NOT REMOVE FLARE.*
3.6.2 or 4.6.2	*Side-slip the butt.*
3.6.3 or 4.6.3	*Wrap.*
3.6.2 or 4.6.4	*Place reed in warm water for 20 minutes.*
3.6.5 or 4.6.5	*Remove reed from water and form tube with parallel mandrel #11 (11/64 inch).*
3.6.6 or 4.6.6	*Unwrap string and put wire III on.*
3.7.6 or 4.6.7	*Remove string and soak string in water.*

3.6.8 or 4.6.8 Mark FFL of 38 mm.

3.6.9 or 4.6.9 Put wire II on.

3.6.10 or 4.6.10 Mold butt.

3.6.11 or 4.6.11 Center-panel molding.

3.6.12 or 4.6.12 Retighten wire II and III.

3.6.13 or 4.6.13 Narrow tip edge to 15.5 mm if needed.

8.8 ADDITIONAL SINK METHOD

If the cane has been gouged according to the Sink Method, then these additional steps are not needed.

a) Let the reed dry for three days or until the wires are loose again.
b) Put the reed back onto the 10/12 mandrel but 2 mm above the mark or, if the reed was formed on the #11 mandrel, put it on the #10 mandrel for tightening the wires. Retighten wires II and III.
c) Straighten the sides with sapphire file if needed.
d) Put on wire I at 26 mm (or at whatever mark is needed for the desired bahn length).
e) Soak reed until it sinks.
f) Dry for three more days.
g) Retighten wires.

3.6.14 or 4.6.14 Adjustment notches.

3.6.15 or 4.6.15 Wrap binding on reed.

3.6.16 or 4.6.16 File the butt of the reed flat so that it can stand vertically.

3.6.17 or 4.6.17 Ream reed with #9 machinist's drill into a depth of 9 mm. Remove bump on the inside with the rattail file.

3.6.18 or 4.6.18 Straighten sides if needed.

3.6.19 or 4.6.19 Cut reed.

3.6.20 or 4.6.20 Adjust side-slipping.

3.6.21 or 4.6.21 Clip corners of reed.

3.6.22 or 4.6.22 Smooth tip edge of reed if needed.

3.6.23 or 4.6.23 Wire I (already done).

3.6.24 or 4.6.24   *Tune reed.*

3.6.25 or 4.6.25   *Glue.*

3.6.26 or 4.6.26   *Dry.*

3.7 or 4.7   *Final Stage*

3.7.1 or 4.7.1   *Tighten wire II around #10 mandrel.*

3.7.2 or 4.7.2   *Tighten wire I.*

3.7.3 or 4.7.3   *Re-ream the tube with #9 machinist's drill in 9 mm. Clean out the shoulder inside the tube with the rat-tail file. (Skinner does not mention the more traditional 3/16 drill bit and file reamer for this step.)*

The tightest case of friction known to man is a cone in a cylinder. We've got a cylindrical tube on the reed which will fit perfectly onto the conical bocal.

CHAPTER 9

A COMPARISON OF THE MECHLER AND KNOCHENHAUER REEDS

The author is in possession of most of Skinner's reed collection, numbering over seventy different examples. For the purposes of this book, data are presented on the Carl Mechler and Wilhelm Knochenhauer reeds that are in the collection, and on examples of reeds by Sherman Walt, Ferdinand Del Negro, and a Straight Taper and Tip Taper reed by Skinner.

Measuring down the centerline, the cane thicknesses in the "Mechler Model" and "Knochenhauer Model" columns of Table 9.1 are averages of both blades of the model reeds shown in Figures 9.1 and 9.2. The thicknesses in the other two columns are averages for four Carl Mechler reeds and five Wilhelm Knochenhauer reeds, including the model reeds. Two Carl Mechler and three Wilhelm Knochenhauer reeds were obtained from Per Hannevold, who received them from Lou Skinner several months before his death. The measurements of Hannevold's reeds were combined with the measurements from two Mechler reeds, and from two Knochenhauer reeds in the author's collection from Skinner, to obtain average blade thicknesses.

The first thing that this table shows is that Skinner used the basic Knochenhauer collar and wire measurements for both the Straight Taper and Tip Taper reeds. In addition, the shape he recommends is very close to the Knochenhauer shape, with the narrowest part of the tube at wire II flaring to the collar, and with straight sides on the blades. Although Mechler's reeds in this collection had straight-sided blades, he was occasionally known to use a convex blade shape that Skinner called *Bavarian*. A brass model of a Bavarian shape resides in Skinner's collection of shapes.

The most important differences between the two reeds are the thickness and slope of the spine. The spines of the Mechler reed (Figure 9.1) slope 0.53 mm down the center of the blades from the collar (1.09 mm) to the midpoint (0.56 mm). In contrast, the slope on the spines of the Knochenhauer reed from the collar to the midpoint is only 0.18 mm (from 0.75 mm to 0.57 mm). Both reeds slope about the same

TABLE 9.1 **Comparison of Mechler and Knochenhauer reeds**

	MECHLER MODEL	MECHLER AVERAGE	KNOCHEN-HAUER MODEL	KNOCHEN-HAUER AVERAGE
Length	59 mm		56 mm	
Collar position	31		30	
Wire I	30		26	
Wire II	22		20	
Width of Tip	14		16	
Width at Collar	8		9.5	
Width at Wire I	8		8	
Width at Wire II	7		7	
BLADE LENGTH	28 (D)		26 (E)	
BAHN LENGTH	29 (C#)		30 (C)	
THICKNESS				
Collar	1.09	1.055	0.75	0.747
35 mm from butt	0.95	0.836	0.69	0.663
43 mm (blade midpoint on Knochenhauer)	0.62	0.65	0.57	0.586
45 mm (blade midpoint on Mechler)	0.56	0.54		
50 mm (6 mm from tip edge on Knochenhauer)	0.47	0.527	0.45	0.444
53 mm (6 mm from tip edge on Mechler)	0.36	0.465		
tip edge (estimated)	0.25	0.25	0.25	0.25
Slope of spines from collar to midpoint of blades	-0.53		-0.18	
Slope of spines from midpoint to tip edge	-0.31		-0.32	

from the midpoint to the tip edge. Relatively speaking, the fibers in the blades of the Mechler reed are much more pyramided over the length of the blades, while the fibers in the blades of the Knochenhauer reed are much more parallel in the back, and pyramided at the tip.

Skinner informed me that the Mechler reed used as the model was made in 1932 and was played in the New York Philharmonic by Benjamin Kohon; it came to Skinner through Otto Eiffert. The reed plays about 25 cents flat on the author's Heckel (#9212) and the one-finger E falls, but the sound has presence and is not dampened.

Skinner said that cane was taken out from the inside of the tip (linear dampening), adding that **many Carl Mechler reeds are gouged thickly because the cane was very hard. A thick gouge meant that the profile could go into softer cane farther from the bark. Much of Carl Mechler's cane was from South America. Carl Mechler made reeds without a collar.**

The Wilhelm Knochenhauer reed (Figure 9.2) has the typical scooped collar and thin blade edges in front of the collar. Unlike the Carl Mechler reed, it is not beveled at the butt. The reed is about 20 cents flat on the author's instrument and plays easily with very little embouchure or breath pressure. The sound is dampened or *dumpf*, as Skinner would say. The higher overtones are lacking, and the one-finger E falls.

Sherman Walt's reed (Figure 9.3) is 56 mm in length with a blade length of 26 mm (E) and a bahn length of 29 mm (C#). The collar is at 30 mm, wire I at 27 mm, and wire II at 17 mm. The butt is beveled. This is very similar to Skinner's Straight Taper model. Skinner mentioned that **Sherman would re-soak his reed until it sank, then dry it thoroughly again and re-tighten the wires** (Section 8.8, "Additional Sink Method"). **This reed is probably from Christlieb cane and has too much out of the heart** (the thickness at 43 mm is 0.64 mm; at 50 mm it is 0.51 mm); **he would take the 50-mm mark down to 0.50 mm immediately.**

Ferdinand Del Negro's reed (Figure 9.4), with 1985 on the wrapping, is 56 mm in length, with the collar at 28 mm, wire I at 27 mm, and wire II at 15 mm. This particular example is 14 mm wide at the tip, probably made narrower by a player. The blade length is 28 mm (D) and the bahn is 29 mm (C#). The back of the reed is heavy (0.95 mm at the collar) and slopes very little to the 43-mm mark (reduced by 0.22 mm to a thickness of 0.73 mm). The blades then drop rapidly to the tip edge, with a thickness of 0.47 at the 50-mm mark. The sides of the blades are trimmed to a knife edge. Skinner said that Del Negro warned him **not to overdo the inside of the tip. One pull of the sand paper was all that was needed. Del gets his lows because of the knife edge and the cane taken out on the sides from the collar to the midpoint.**

The final two models are Skinner's: a Straight Taper model that he sometimes called his *Walt* reed, and a Tip Taper model which he referred to as his *Del* model (the Del-model process is described in Section 8.1). (Photographs of these two models appear in Figure 9.5 and Figure 9.6, and their measurements are given in Table 9.2.)

There are two main differences between the two reeds: their profiles and their placement of wire I. The thickness at the collar of the Straight Taper reed is 0.90 mm, while the thickness at the collar of the Tip Taper reed is 0.80 mm. Both are roughly 0.65 mm thick halfway down the blades, at the 43 mm mark. Therefore, the slope on the Straight Taper reed from the collar to the midpoint is 0.25 mm, while the slope on the Tip Taper reed is a more parallel 0.15 mm. Because the Tip Taper reed has a bahn length of 27 mm and a natural low pitch of E flat, Skinner removed cane from the "No Man's Land" area of the mid-range, from the collar to the midpoint of the blades (Figure 7.1). The edges are also knife-edge thin. Skinner said that he **used an outside trim** on the Del model **and a 2 mm or 3 mm** *brevis* **so that he could have a wider tip.**

The sound of the two reeds is completely different. The Straight Taper model has plenty of overtones and a presence or center to the sound, but verges on being buzzy. The Tip Taper model had a rounder wire I and was darker with a more covered sound, but without the presence or center of the Straight Taper reed.

TABLE 9.2 **Comparison of Skinner's Straight Taper (Walt) model with his Tip Taper (Del) model**

CHARACTERISTIC	STRAIGHT TAPER: WALT MODEL	TIP TAPER: DEL NEGRO MODEL
Length	56 mm	56 mm
Collar position	30	30
Wire I	26	29
Wire II	18	18
Width of Tip	15	15
Width at Collar	8	8
Width at Wire I	7.5	7
Width at Wire II	7	7
Width at Butt	7	7
BLADE LENGTH	26 (E)	26 (E)
BAHN LENGTH	30 (C)	27 (E flat)
THICKNESS[32]		
collar	0.90/0.88	0.80/0.80
35 mm	0.70/0.70	0.76/0.76
43 mm	0.66/0.62	0.65/0.64
50 mm	0.50/0.48	0.51/0.51
tip	0.25/0.25	0.25/0.25
Slope from collar to midpoint	0.24/0.26	0.15/0.15

As you can see from the measurements of the two models, both, in fact, are hybrids of the basic processes. Skinner also made a reed that had a Tip Taper profile but incorporated Four Flats (Section 5.3) and Even Down Around Shape (Section 6.5); he achieved the necessary dampening and trim on the inside of the blades but purposely did not do a tip undercut. This reed had the dark quality of the Tip Taper but gave more upper overtones.

Finally, Skinner told me that in the late 1980s he profiled all his cane with a Straight Taper on one machine and only *added* a Tip Taper to the Straight Taper from his other

---

32. The thicknesses are given with wire I up to the left of the slash (/) and wire I down to the right of the slash.

profiler. In fact, Skinner's profilers, which the author received along with the reeds and other tools, were set up to do precisely what he described, although they made heavier profiles than those described in this book.

The only caution that he had was to make sure that the Tip Taper profile started at the 50-mm mark on the blades.[33] You could use two machines, or a double-sloping template. Also use a 3-mm *brevis* to give yourself a wider tip.

---

33. Skinner means that the Tip Taper should be added by the profiling machine at 50 mm. However, by the time that the reed is finished, that slope will have been moved back to approximately 45 mm, as described in Figure 3.1.

CHAPTER 10

THE CONTRABASSOON REED

Construction of the contrabassoon reed follows closely that of the bassoon reeds presented in Chapters 3 and 4. Because of the larger size of the contrabassoon reed, the harmonics of the crow reverse, with the C sounding as the high pitch and the F as the low pitch. The pitch of the crows remains dependent on the blade length and bahn length. Much the same as with the bassoon reed, when the bahn is shortened the low pitch rises. However, in contrast to the bassoon reed, when the blade length is shortened the high pitch is lowered. Table 10.1 illustrates these relationships.

TABLE 10.1 **Effect of blade and bahn lengths on the natural pitches of the contrabassoon reed crow, assuming that the reed is 19 to 20 mm wide at the tip**

LOWS		HIGHS	
Bahn	Pitch	Blade	Pitch
37 mm	F	30 mm	C
36 mm	G flat	31 mm	B
35 mm	G	32 mm	B flat
34 mm	A flat	33 mm	A
33 mm	A	34 mm	A flat
		35 mm	G

The following instructions refer to the construction of a 66-mm long contrabassoon reed with a 33-mm blade length and 36-mm bahn.

98   Chapter 10

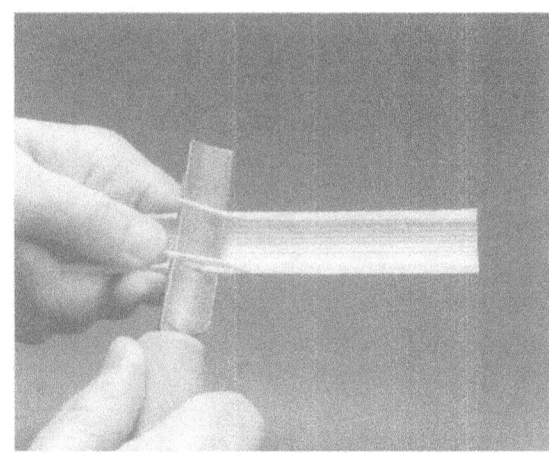

FIGURE 10.1
Cutting off edges of cane

10.1 PREPARATION OF TUBES, GOUGING, AND PROFILING

10.1.1 *Split the cane longitudinally into three parts*

The tube of cane should be straight, 150 mm long or longer, and 28 mm in outside diameter. Mark the tube on one end, designating three equal sections. Score each mark and split the cane at each mark with the grain: using a heavy knife, press downward onto the end of the tube while it is supported vertically on the bench.

10.1.2 *Soak the cane (the Sink Method)*

Soak the cane until it sinks (about five days) and change the water each day, keeping it covered. Besides softening the cane, soaking leaches out sap and impurities. After five days the water should remain clear. Drain the water and leave the cane covered for two more days.

10.1.3 *Cut cane to 137 mm in length for gouging machine*

Cut a piece of drained cane to 137 mm in length using a guillotine cutter or a sharp pair of pruning shears.

10.1.4 *Cut off sharp edges (fillier)*

Holding one end of the piece of cane, cut edges off each side (Figure 10.1), producing flats on each edge of the inside of the tube. Reverse the cane and repeat on the other end, so that the flats are consistent across the entire length of the cane. The cane should then fit in the gouger with the flats aligned with the top surface of the gouger bed.

10.1.5 *Gouge cane*

Gouge the cane while it is still wet; the gouge should be eccentric, approximately

1.50 mm (±0.05 mm) in thickness in the center. After gouging, the cane can be dried on a 1-1/4-inch dowel and stored.

10.1.6 *Profile cane (with profiling machine)*

There are two methods for removing the bark between the collar marks: *profiling by machine* and *profiling by hand.* The machine method is outlined here.

Profiling can be performed on a standard single-barrel Pfeifer profiler. The cane will overhang the easel by 5 mm on each end. The cane should be profiled by machine while it is wet; the profile should have no side-to-side variation. This is ensured by placing the pins on the profiling easel so that the flats do not affect the profile. The profiler should be set to have a blade length beginning 36 mm from the butt end. The thickness should be 0.50 mm at the fold and 0.90 mm just before the radius left at the collar (Figure 10.2).

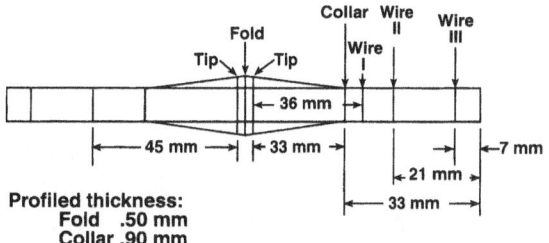

FIGURE 10.2
Profile for the contrabassoon reed

Let the cane dry; it takes 12 hours to dry at room temperature, 6 hours in a warming oven or a gas oven with a pilot light, or 20 minutes directly under a 60-watt lamp. Using wet cane for the next steps is inadvisable, since drying causes shrinkage, making the measurements inaccurate.

Using a #32 scraper, lightly scrape the inside of the gouge to level the grain that rose during the soaking and drying.

Sand the inside with 280 WD sandpaper, leave the dust, and repeat the sanding procedure with the smooth paper side of the sandpaper. Rubbing the sanding dust into the grain of the cane with the back of the sandpaper will polish the inside gouged surface.

10.2 SHAPING AND PRE-TRIM

10.2.1 *Making a masking-tape shaper template*

In his earlier days of reed making, Lou Skinner experimented extensively with different shapes. He shaped his cane as described here using brass shim stock and masking tape. This is a very effective way to shape cane when you do not have a standard folding or straight shaper. The technique presented here can be applied in making either bassoon or contrabassoon reeds.

The contrabassoon reed shape is illustrated in Figure 10.3. Using 0.60 mm brass shim stock, cut a template that matches the shape in Figure 10.3; this will form the basis for all reed shaping.

Fold two layers of 1-inch-wide masking tape over the brass template and press to adhere to the template. Cut off excess masking tape with scissors (Figure 10.4). Remove the tape and place it on the cane, with the center line of the shape lying over the center line of the gouged cane (Figure 10.5).

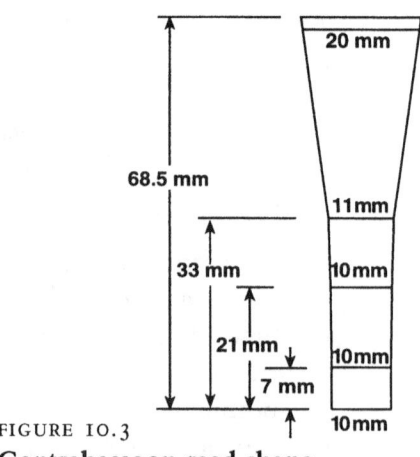

FIGURE 10.3
Contrabassoon reed shape

10.2.2 *Shaping the cane*

With a sharp #10 Exacto knife, cut off excess cane. Be careful not to undercut the cane inside the borders of the shape. Hold the cane in the left hand with one edge up, making sure that your left hand is below the edge of the tape template (left-handed people, of course, use opposite hands). Begin by placing the blade just beyond the widest point of the shape and cut along the grain away from you and toward the butt end, cutting away a piece 2 mm to 3 mm thick. Continue to *feather* the cane back to the butt end until you have replicated the shape of the template.

Repeat on the three remaining sides (or quadrants). Remove the tape by pulling it away from each end and toward the center so you can save it for shaping the next piece of cane. A tape template is usually good for shaping three reeds.

10.2.3 *Mark collar and wire positions*

With a pair of machine dividers, mark the points as shown in Figure 10.2, always measuring from the butt end. If necessary, enlarge the marks with a knife-edge file by scoring transversely across the cane for each wire and collar. Wire III is 7 mm from the butt, Wire II is at 21 mm, and the collar is at 33 mm.

10.3 OMIT WINDSOR MILL PROCESS

10.4 CENTER-PANEL SCORING

10.4.1 *Define center panel and cut scores on tube ends*

With machine dividers, draw a small line on the bark of the tube, parallel to the sides, inset 4 mm from each side, and running from the collar to the butt end.

Score the cane along each 4-mm mark to the butt end. To do this, use the tip of an Exacto knife to penetrate the bark lightly in a line running down and past

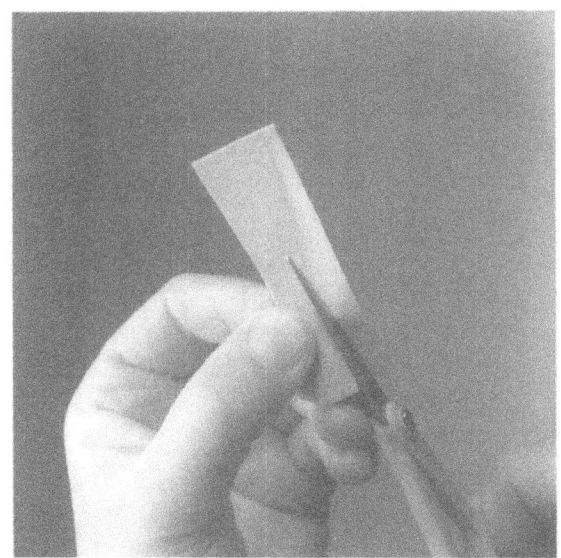

FIGURE 10.4
Double layer of masking tape folded over the brass template, with excess tape being cut away

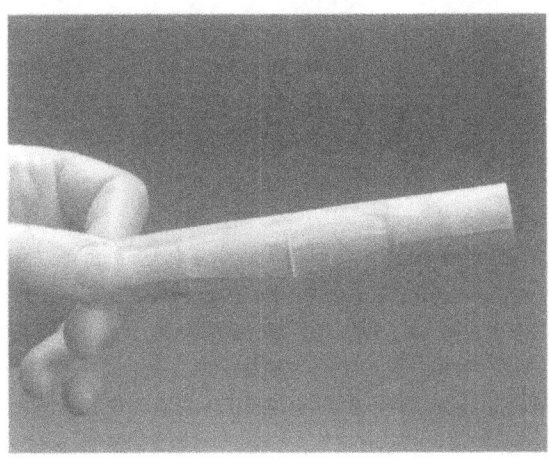

FIGURE 10.5
Shaped masking tape placed on the profiled cane

the butt at right angles to the collar. This is most easily accomplished if you place the cane on a 1-1/4-inch easel and the easel on the table. Score three more lines, parallel to the first, progressively closer to the edge of the cane.

It is essential that the score lines are all the same depth and run parallel. The scoring need be only deep enough to penetrate the bark (about 0.20 mm). For the final 1 mm at the butt end of each score line, press the Exacto blade right through the cane. If the score marks are not parallel and even in depth, the tube will form unevenly when the mandrel is inserted, causing pressure ridges and ruining the balance in the blades. The tube could even split into the blades, causing an irreparable air leak.

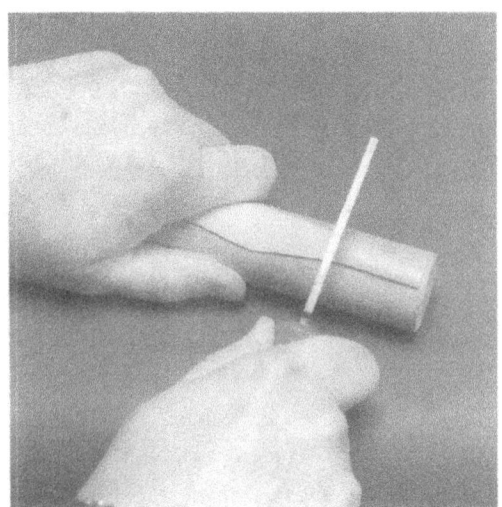
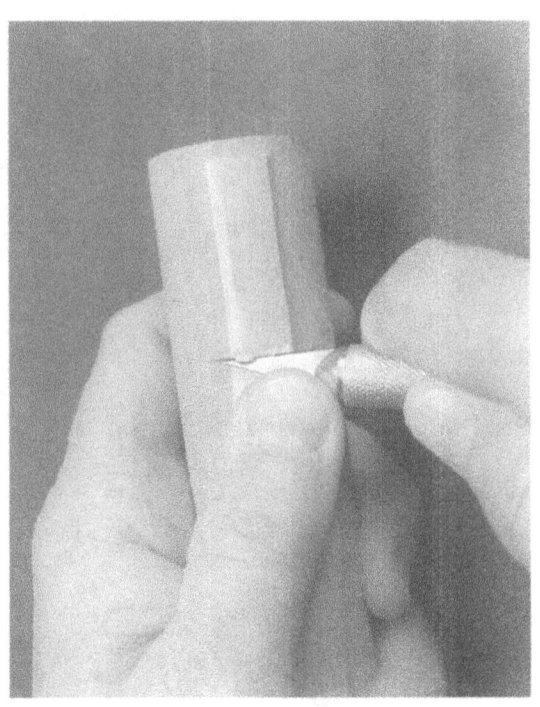

FIGURE 10.6 *(above)*
Cutting in the collar
FIGURE 10.7 *(right)*
Undercutting the profile radius at the collar

10.4.2 *Cut in collar*

Place the cane on an easel 1-1/4-inch in diameter and score transversely with 20 double strokes along the collar marks with a sharp knife or a knife-edge file, cutting through almost one-half of the thickness of the cane (Figure 10.6). After scoring, hold the cane on the easel and cut the profiled radius at the collar back to the collar score mark by undercutting the bark with a #11 Exacto knife. Cut from the parallel profiled surface back to the scoring while keeping the profile thickness constant (Figure 10.7). Smooth out the undercutting with a sapphire file with ten transverse strokes, working across the cane from one side to the other. Repeat ten strokes working in the reverse transverse direction. Feather in the sapphire file marks by making a few strokes of the file along the grain of the cane.

10.5 PRE-TRIM

The sides of the reed need to be reduced by about 0.10 mm in thickness. Place the profiled cane on an easel and with a knife scrape ten double strokes (down and back) on each side of the profiled surface. Start at the collar and scrape toward the fold. The scrape should have a width of 1 mm, lying along the edge of the cane. Use 280 WD to blend the resulting ridge into the blades.

Sand ten double strokes (down and back) on the wings from the collar to the fold about 3 mm from the edge.

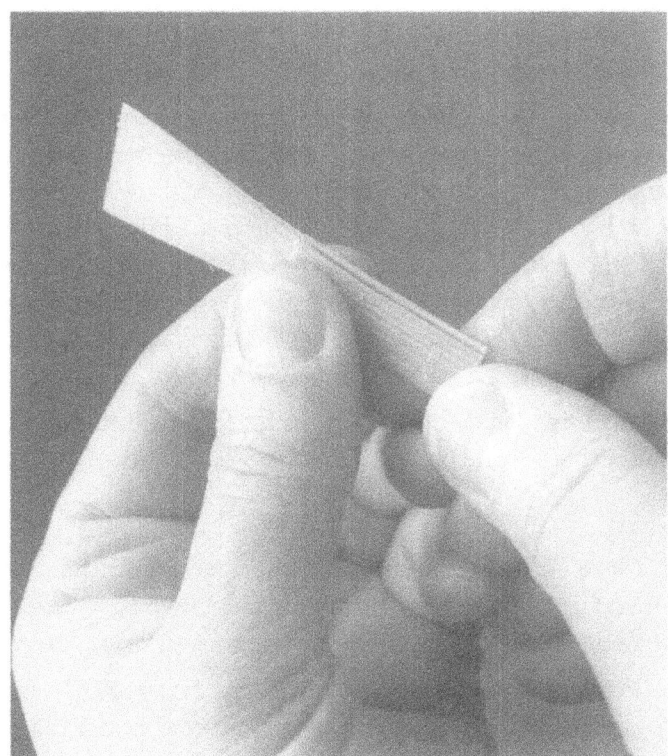

FIGURE 10.8
Folding the cane with 1-mm side-slip

With 400 WD, lightly sand the entire blade surface to smooth out the scraping and previous sanding strokes.

10.6 FORMING AND DRYING

10.6.1 Mark and score the center for folding

Using a divider or ruler, locate the center of the cane and mark it for the fold. Using a knife or a knife-edge file, score transversely across the cane with ten single strokes at the mark. Be careful not to cut through the cane.

10.6.2 Bevel cane

Holding the cane with the profiled side up, bevel the right side underneath edge starting at the collar and beveling to the butt end. The angle of bevel should be a maximum of 45 degrees from perpendicular to the cane surface (Section 5.5).

10.6.3 Soak and fold cane

Soak the cane in hot water (just under boiling) for 20 minutes. Remove and fold at the center score. Side-slip the two halves so that the top half of the butt end slips to the left of the bottom half by approximately 1 mm (Figure 10.8). This procedure allows the blades to fit together better because they will be slightly overlapped. The effect of the 1 mm side-slip will be lessened when the forming mandrel is inserted and turned clockwise.

Wrap dry, standard cotton crochet thread (starting 5 mm below the collar) down to the butt end. This wrapping is essential so that the tube of the reed will be formed evenly. Use the same cotton crochet thread that you will use to finish wrapping the reed. Begin by laying the standing end of the thread on the upper side of the tube at the collar and wrapping two courses or revolutions over it. This should secure the thread. Continue wrapping carefully and tightly toward the butt end, making sure each course is laid evenly beside the previous course. Do not allow any course to override a neighboring course. Finish with a slipknot.

Place the reed and string back in the near-boiling water for four minutes. Heat the #13 pin mandrel in the water for the last 30 seconds.

10.6.4 *Form tube*

Remove reed from water. Place #13 pin mandrel into the aperture of the butt end and slowly but firmly insert, gently twisting the mandrel clockwise as needed, up to the mark, or until the edges of the cane at the butt just begin to separate.

Begin by grasping the reed with thumb and forefinger on the sides of the wire III mark. Start pushing the mandrel in gently at first. Make sure that the mandrel goes in straight and not at an angle. Pushing the mandrel in at an angle could cause one side of the tube to arch and crack more than the other. A certain amount of cracking is almost inevitable in the tube. The cracking may extend into the blade, but as long as the crack remains on the surface of the cane and does not go right through, the reed is salvageable. Any pressure ridges that are created because of a crack in the surface of the tube must be taken care of in the final trim by removing cane from the blade at the point in the collar where the split enters the blade.

10.6.5 *Place wire III on tube*

Partially unwrap the string from the butt end to just beyond the wire III mark (Figure 10.9). Pull the string counterclockwise to maintain the tension of the slipknot. Put wire III on, using #21 soft brass wire. Holding the reed on the mandrel, wrap the wire counterclockwise two full turns,[34] moving up the tube toward the blade and making sure that the courses are adjacent and not overlapping.

With your fingers, twist both ends of the wire counterclockwise one or two full turns. Tighten with pliers by pulling the twisted wire away from the tube, and

---

34. Skinner considered a "full turn" to be one complete revolution of the wires accomplished with the fingers. A "full twist" is a 1/4 turn, using pliers. A "half twist" is therefore 1/8 of a turn, using pliers.

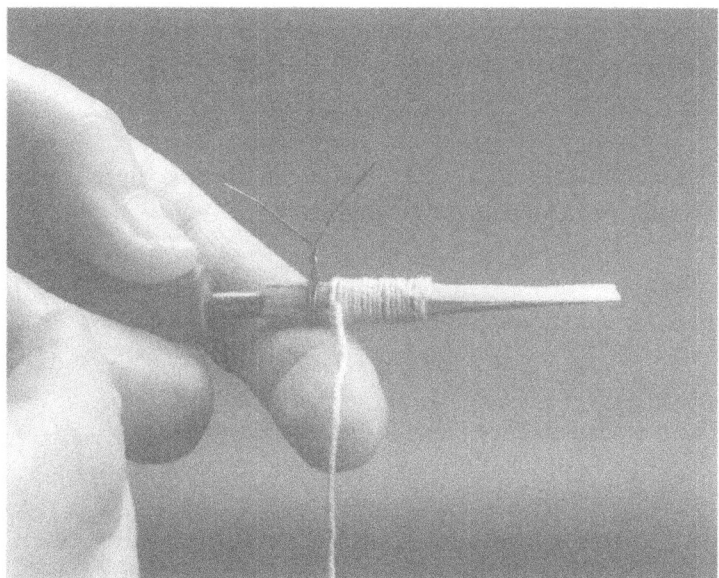

FIGURE 10.9 **Placing wire III on the tube**

twisting counterclockwise to snug; four or five full twists should be sufficient. Always pull to tighten and twist to snug. Clip off excess wire above the second twist.

Remove the string up to the second mark. With a pencil compass, place a mark on the blade 45 mm from the second wire mark. This indicates where the tip will be cut.

10.6.6 *Place wire II on tube*

Follow the same procedures as in Step 10.6.5, but make sure that the twist of wire II is on the opposite side of the tube from wire III. Pull to tighten, twist (counterclockwise) to lock. Cut the wire twist, leaving 6 mm, measured from the cane.

10.6.7 *Remove string and soak string in water*

Soak the cotton string first: later, when the string has been put back on the reed and dries, it will shrink tightly around the tube, helping to make a well-formed airtight tube.

10.6.8 *File in adjustment notches*

With the knife-edge file, cut in adjustment notches (four or five of them) between wires III and II, on the center panels, and on the sides of the tube. Adjustment notches are essential for later alterations to the tube between wires II and III, and these alterations will affect response and pitch.

10.6.9 Straighten the sides

With a sapphire file aligned with the edge of the blade, file the edge lightly with ten double strokes to straighten the edge of the blade.

10.6.10 Wrap turk's head

While the reed and string are wet, wrap the turk's head on the reed.

10.6.11 File butt end

File the butt end of the reed flat so that reed can stand vertically.

10.6.12 Ream the reed with the drill and file reamers

Using a 7/32-inch drill, ream the butt end. Push the drill in, twisting clockwise to a depth of 22 mm. Using a 5/16-inch file reamer, file the reamed hole. The file reamer is inserted 22 mm, twisting counterclockwise. Use of these tools can be facilitated by putting tape on the shafts as stops at the appropriate distances. Finish by filing the inside of the butt with a small rattail file to smooth out the inside surface and remove any filings and roughness left from the reaming.

10.6.13 Align sides

If the sides of the shape have twisted apart as a result of the reaming, realign them by twisting wire III or by straightening the sides again with sapphire file.

10.6.14 Cut reed

This can be done with a knife and cutting block, with a pair of large pruning sheers, or with a tip cutter. Cut reed at Full Fundamental Length: 45 mm from wire II.

10.6.15 Adjust side-slipping

To ensure that the reed does not leak, adjust the side-slipping of the blades so that the upper right side is slightly inside lower right when viewed from the butt end.

10.6.16 Clip corners of reed and smooth tip edge

The angle of the corners of the reed should be 45 degrees, and not more than 1 mm long. Using a sapphire file at right angles to the blade surface, very lightly file the corners with single strokes that move away from the reed tip. Do not file the corner back toward the reed, as this will split the edge of the cane.

Holding the aperture closed with your thumb and index finger, and with the sapphire file at right angles to the blade surface, continue to file lightly across the tip edge until it is smooth (Steps 3.7.5 and 4.7.5).

10.6.17 Crow the reed

Lightly crow the reed to determine the highest crow pitch. With the dimensions of the reed length and blade described here, the pitch should be near A-440.

10.6.18 Place wire I on the tube

Put wire I on loosely between wire II and collar. Slide it and secure it 36 mm from the tip edge. The bahn length (distance from wire I to the tip edge) for this reed is 36 mm. Measurement should be made from the side of wire I closest to the tip edge. Tighten wire I to a snug but not tight position. Do not bend the twist down. Ensure that the twist of wire I is on the same side of the tube as the twist of wire III and that it has been turned counterclockwise, like wires II and III.

10.6.19 Glue tube

Put two coats of glue on the tube up to just below the wire I. Allow 20 minutes between coats. You can also add colored dope or nail polish.

10.6.20 Let reed dry

The drying process should take 48 hours naturally, or 12 hours if the reed is placed in an electric oven at the *warming* temperature of 65°C (150°F), or in a gas oven with a pilot light.

10.7 FINAL STAGE

10.7.1 Tighten wire II

Tighten wire II by pulling and twisting counterclockwise. Clip wire II to binding and wire I to three twists. You will hear a cracking sound as the seal created by the cement around wire II is broken. File off the sharp edges of the wires.

10.7.2 Tighten wire I

Grasp wire I with pliers and allow the reed to settle into the mark made during forming. Make sure that the bahn length is still 36 mm. Tighten wire I by pulling and locking with two full twists. If wire I is still loose, tighten with one more half-twist. Fold wire I over toward butt, and file off sharp edges.

Wire I should not move when the reed is dry. However, if wire I is too tight, it may cause the reed to be restricted in its vibrations. In this case, wire I should be replaced.

NOTE: A *full-twist* is a quarter turn, and a *half-twist* is an eighth of a turn.

10.7.3 Re-ream the tube

Use the drill reamer first, then the file reamer as in Step 10.6.12. The tube has dried and shrunk since the first reaming and therefore must be reamed again. Use a rattail file to remove loose fibers from inside the tube.

10.7.4 Correct side-slipping

If the tip edge has side-slipped, hold the reed at wire III and twist at wire I in the opposite direction of the side-slip.

10.7.5 Straighten sides

Straighten the sides, renew the corners, and polish the tip edge with the sapphire file.

10.8 FINAL TRIM

10.8.1 Finish sanding the reed tip and blade surface

Place a metal plaque in the tip and lightly sand the tip edge with 280 WD, keeping the sandpaper paper mostly on the plaque. Use ten double strokes at the center and ten on each side on each blade (Figure 3.16). Lightly sand the surface of the whole blade.

10.8.2 Apply tip undercut (Darmstadt tip)

Cut a piece of 320 WD sandpaper 8 mm wide and 5 cm long. Insert the sandpaper strip into the tip of the reed approximately 30 mm in the center of the reed. Hold the tip together and pull the sandpaper out once. Repeat on the right and left sides. Turn the sandpaper around and repeat on the opposite blade. This is the most important step of the contrabassoon reed making process (Figure 3.15).

10.8.3 Test the reed

Skinner intended that the contrabassoon reed be tested on a bassoon. To accomplish this, place one thickness of transparent tape on the end of the bocal to prevent air leaking. The reed will play a half-step flat.

10.8.4 Adjust the reed

Adjust the reed as you would a regular bassoon reed. If the reed is stiff, take cane off lightly on the sides and back. If the reed is undampened and the low notes rattle, carefully thin the wings. Figures 10.10 and 10.11 show photographs of one of Skinner's contrabassoon reeds, made in 1990.

Table 10.2 provides critical measurements of that reed.

TABLE 10.2 **Measurements of one of Skinner's contrabassoon reeds, made in 1990**

Length	66 mm
Collar position	34
Wire I	32
Wire II	21
Width of tip	20
Width at collar	10
Width at wire I	9.5
Width at wire II	8
Width at butt	7.5
Blade length	32
Bahn length	34
Thicknesses*	
Collar	0.94/0.93
40	0.91/0.90
45	0.80/0.78
50 (halfway on the blade)	0.77/0.72
55	0.69/0.66
@ 55 and 4 mm laterally	0.60/0.63 (left & right of 60 mm averaged)
60	0.56/0.57
@ 60 and 4 mm laterally	0.53/0.52 (left & right of 60 mm averaged)
Tip	0.29/0.30

* Thicknesses to the left of the slash (/) are for the blade, with wire I, *up*; thicknesses to the right of the slash are for the the blade, with wire I, *down*. All thicknesses are on the centerline (except those noted as lateral measurements) and are measured from the butt end.

SOURCES

Thomas Elliott, "Reed Notes from My Study with Lou Skinner, 1985-1989." (Notes on reed styles and variations, based on studies with Louis Skinner; corrected by Skinner.)

Russell Hinkle, "Notes on Contrabassoon Reed Making." (Notes based on studies with Louis Skinner; corrected by Skinner.)

James Keyes, "Notes on Contrabassoon Reed Making." (Notes based on studies with Louis Skinner; corrected by Skinner.)

James McKay, audio tape and notes from interviews with Louis Skinner. (More than twenty hours of audio tape and notes from August 1990, recorded by McKay and reviewed by Skinner.)

James McKay, Bill Woodward, and Gerald Corey. "The Skinner Concept of Bassoon Reeds." (Handout from lecture at 1994 International Double Reed Society Conference, Bloomington, Indiana.)

Louis Skinner, "Excerpts from My Shop Notes." (Fourteen pages of diagrams to go with "Notes 1985." Used as handouts for private students and at seminars at York University in 1985 and 1986.)

———, "Notes 1985." (Six-page handout, distributed like his "Excerpts from My Shop Notes.")

GLOSSARY

Adjustment notches — Four or five notches put into the top, bottom, and sides of the tube between wires II and III to allow the tube to be reshaped after the reed has been finished. The adjustments control the aperture. (Figure 1.1).

Aperture — The opening of the reed through which one blows.

Backbone — That part of the finished reed down the center in the high-range area extending from the collar and blending into the heart (Figure 7.1). Also called the "spine."

Bahn length — The measurement from in front of wire I to the tip edge (Figure 1.1).

Bevel — A progressive angle of the abutting edges of the tube (*see* Section 5.5).

Blade length — The measurement from the collar to the tip edge (Figure 1.1).

Brevis — Removal of 2 or 3 mm of cane from the ends of a profiled and shaped piece of cane (described in Step 6.1.1).

Butt end — The part of the reed that fits onto the bocal (Figure 1.1).

Capo d'astro — Wire I, the tuning wire (Figure 1.1).

Chattering — Uneven (and undesirable) skid-like removal of cane when the knife keeps sticking and slipping.

Dampening — Making the reed more resistant to vibration. See also "Horizontal dampening" and "Linear dampening." (Discussed at beginning of Chapter 1.)

DRY — Type of sandpaper intended to be used only dry, not wet.

FFL — Full fundamental length. The distance from wire I to the tip edge (page 5).

Fillier	Removing the sharp edges of the cane prior to placing it onto the gouger (Step 3.1.4).
Fluting or *flutes*	A gouge enhancement that removes cane from the inside of the reed, parallel to the bark and generally from the center of the tube, parallel to the fibers (Section 6.3). *See also* Resonance cuts.
Fulcrum	Wire II (Figure 1.1).
HD	Abbreviation for "horizontal dampening" or "horizontally dampened."
Heart area	Section of the finished reed between the 43 mm to 50 mm marks (measuring from the butt end), in the high- and mid-range areas of the blades (Figure 7.1).
Horizontal dampening	Reed style in which the largest amount of dampening by the embouchure to close the aperture is lateral or from side-to-side on the blades. Typical of Tip Taper reeds (page 3). The procedures used to achieve horizontal dampening are carried out on the outside of the blades.
LD	Abbreviation for "linear dampening" or "linearly dampened."
LE	Abbreviation for "linear enhancement" or "linearly enhanced."
Linear dampening	Reed style in which the largest amount of dampening by the embouchure to close the aperture is longitudinal or from the collar of the reed to the tip. Typical of Straight Taper reeds (page 3). The procedures used to achieve linear dampening are carried out on the inside of the blades (Chapter 6).
Linear enhancement	Change made to the inside of the blades, making them taper from the collar to the tip edge (Section 6.1).
"No Man's Land"	Area of the finished reed, from the collar to 43 mm in the mid-range area on either side of the backbone (Figure 7.1).
Pressure ridge	A crack that appears on the outer surface of the bark in the tube. If it extends into the blade, a leak may occur. (Sections 3.4d and 4.4d.)
Profile	The shape of a reed when viewed in lengthwise cross-section.
Pyramided fibers	A thickening of cane in the blades (Figure 1.3), resulting from a diagonal cut through several layers of fiber.
Resiliency	The force that causes the cane to return to its original curvature (Section 1.3).

Resistance	The dampening of vibrations due to pyramided fibers (Section 1.3).
Resonance cuts	A gouge enhancement or type of fluting that removed cane from the inside of a reed, parallel to the bark and generally across the fibers along the sides of the blades (Section 6.3, "The Vivaldi Reed"). The effect of this gouge enhancement is to increase the space on the inside of the reed, and to free up the vibrations, hence increasing the resonance of the reed. *See also* Fluting.
Scraping wheel or scraper	Steel disk with a sharpened edge, used to remove cane from the inside of the gouge (Section 2.1).
Spine	*See* Backbone.
Tip edge	The part of the reed that forms the aperture (Figure 1.1).
Tube	The part of the reed from the collar to the butt end (Figure 1.1).
Twist	*Full twist:* 1/4 turn on wire I.
	Half twist: 1/8 turn on wire I (Step 3.7.2).
Variation	A procedure that may have specific benefits but is not indispensable when making a reed.
WD	Type of sandpaper that can be used either Wet or Dry.

James R. McKay maintains an active schedule as a bassoonist, conductor, acoustic researcher, university professor, and adjudicator. He appears on more than a dozen recordings with artists including James Campbell, Anton Kuerti, Steven Staryk, and Ofra Harnoy, and with ensembles including the Festival of the Sound, the Amadeus Ensemble, and the Contemporary Chamber Players of Chicago. He is frequently featured as a soloist or conductor in broadcast concerts on CBC, CJRT, PBS, and in many North American music festivals. He is a founding member of the York Winds, Triptych, and the Poulenc Ensemble and has toured as a soloist and chamber musician in Canada, the United States, Japan, and Europe. McKay studied bassoon with Leonard Sharrow, Ferdinand Del Negro, and Nicholas Kilburn, and reed making with Louis Skinner. Professor McKay is the Chair of the Department of Music Performance Studies in the Faculty of Music at the University of Western Ontario, and Music Director of Symphony Hamilton.

Russell Hinkle served as Principal Bassoon with the Dayton Philharmonic from 1953 to his retirement in 1995. He performed with the former Dayton Opera Orchestra for thirty-six years, and he was Principal Bassoon for three years with the Cincinnati Opera Orchestra. He has performed with numerous area orchestras, including the Springfield, Hamilton, Richmond, Cincinnati, and Indianapolis Symphonies. Hinkle studied bassoon with Hans A. R. Meuser, and reed making with Louis Skinner. He is retired Band Director of Mt. Healthy High School in Cincinnati and holds a Bachelor of Music Degree from the University of Cincinnati, College-Conservatory of Music.

William Woodward resides in Greensburg, Pennsylvania and currently performs as a freelance musician in the greater Pittsburgh area, playing with the Altoona and McKeesport Symphonies, as well as with several chamber groups. He is also the proprietor of Custom Cane, a business that sells bassoon cane processed according to Louis Skinner's methods. He earned a bachelor's degree in mechanical engineering from the University of Delaware and his M.S. and Ph.D. in mechanical engineering from the University of Pennsylvania. During that time he freelanced in the Philadelphia area, playing with the Wilmington Symphony (now the Delaware Symphony), the Pennsylvania Pro Musica and the Philadelphia Orchestra Society. Woodward studied bassoon with Ferdinand Del Negro, Leonard Sharrow, Artemus Edwards, and Stephen Paulson, and reed making with Louis Skinner.